The History and Art of the Russian Icon

Inquiries should be addressed to: Siamese Imports Co., Inc., 148 Plandome Rd., Manhasset, N.Y. 11030.

Library of Congress Cataloging-in-Publication Data

Vorob'ev, Nikolai Aleksandrovich, 1922–the history and art of the Russian icon from the X to the XX centuries.

1. Icons, Russian. 2. Icon painting—Russian S.F.S.R. I. Ginzburg, George A. II. Maxym, Lucy. III. Title.
N8189.S62R978 1986 755'.2 86-60498

ISBN 0-940202-06-9

Printed in the United States of America

THE HISTORY AND ART OF THE RUSSIAN ICON

FROM THE X TO THE XX CENTURIES

Russian Text By Nikolai A. Vorobyev
Translated By Boris M. Meerovich

Photography By George A. Ginzburg

Book Designed By Mikhail A. Anikst

Commissioned and Edited by Lucy Maxym

Introduction

In the winter of 1984, during a routine trip to Moscow in connection with my importation of Russian Lacquer boxes and antique Russian icons, I met Mr. George Ginzburg, who was assigned to photograph me for an article which was being written on the occasion of the 50th anniversary of the Government Agency through which I purchased these objects of art.

During the photography session, we talked about my interest in Russian art in general, and antique icons in particular, and about the success of a book which I had written and published on Russian Lacquer, Legends and Fairy Tales. He told me that he had seen my book and liked it very much and asked if I planned to publish any other books dealing with Russian art. I answered that it had always been my dream to publish a book on Russian icons.

I told Mr. Ginzburg that for many years I had been involved in personal appearances in many fine stores throughout my country in connection with the sale of both the lacquer and icons. My experience was that although there was an enormous interest in the icons, it was a rather mysterious subject about which very little was really known by the general public in the United States. After looking at the beautiful displays of icons, many people would invariably come up to me and ask—sometimes quite shyly as though they should know better—"Exactly what *is* an Icon?" It was obvious of course that all the icons had one thing in common—the religious subject matter. But what these people wanted to know was more than that. Why and how were they made in that particular way? Why were they so different from paintings made for other religions? Who were the painters, what were their names, and which were the most famous? Why weren't the icons signed? What were the "covers" which decorated so many of them and why were they put there? What was under those "covers" which allowed only the faces, hands and feet of the subjects of the paintings to be seen? How could one be sure that an icon was authentic and really from the period in which it was supposed to have been painted? The questions went on and on—the curiosity of those who came to look at the icons seemed endless. I tried my best to answer them as completely as I could. I knew that, except in very scholarly and complicated texts which sometimes made for difficult reading, certainly for a layman who had no prior knowledge of either icons or the Russian Orthodox religion, it was difficult to find information on the subject in existing books in the English language.

Therefore, when Mr. Ginzburg asked me if I thought of publishing any other books, I answered that I had given a great deal of thought to publishing a book, in English, which would answer the question—What is an Icon?—in a clear, interesting and reliable way; a book which would cover the history and art of icon painting and how it evolved under the conditions of ancient Russian society, the techniques involved in the actual creation and painting of an icon, descriptions of the men who painted them, an explanation of the pictorial "language" of the icon, its symbolism, its subject matter, and the overall role that the icon played in the lives of the people who revered them. Alas, I did not consider myself sufficiently authoritative on this subject to write the text. Also, in order to have an interesting book, it would be necessary to include fine reproductions of the most important examples of this art from the eleventh to the beginning of the twentieth century—an almost impossible task for me since these works of art were in various museums scattered throughout the length and breadth of the Soviet Union, as well as in private collections to which I did not have access. It would be a herculean task, taking years, to try to arrange for the completion of such a project.

Our photography session now long over, Mr. Ginzburg and I talked on for several hours. It was obvious that he was fascinated with the entire idea. Suddenly, he said—"We could do it!" and asked if I was indeed prepared to publish such a book if everything that I needed could be done. Would I be interested in meeting with two colleagues of his—a book designer who was considered to be one of the best in his field, as well as an icon specialist who could write the text?

And so the project was born... That very evening, Mikhail Anikst, George Ginzburg and I sat around a table, drinking cup after cup of strong Russian tea, and ideas swirled around between us like snowflakes on a wintry Moscow night! Before the evening was over, the title for the book (which I had been carrying around somewhere in the back of my mind for years) was agreed upon, Mikhail Anikst had sketched out the cover design as well as a preliminary plan for the actual size and the general "look" of the book, a discussion of the kinds of photographs we needed to include as well as the scope of the photographic coverage was decided upon, and many other matters including the style of type we wanted down to the weight and appearance of the paper to be used were gone into in great detail.

The next order of business was to meet with the Fine Arts Department of the Copyright Agency of the U.S.S.R., through whom the work would be done, and then to have a long meeting with their colleague, Nicolai Vorobyev, who, they both assured me, was eminently qualified to write the text.

The meeting with the Copyright Agency took place the next day and was most cordial. After my meeting with Mr. Vorobyev, I was convinced that the text was in the best of hands. He understood exactly what I wanted and promised that he would undertake the writing of the text from the point of view that I suggested.

I left Moscow the next day. I remember thinking on the plane that I hoped nothing would stand in the way of the completion and publication of the book, and thinking also that just three short days before I had not even known the people with whom I would be working so closely on this project!

When I returned to Moscow some six months later, we all met again. Many of the photographs had already been completed—and they were exciting! George Ginzburg had traveled extensively that winter to obtain photographs of "Russian Churches in the Snow" which I had insisted had to be included in the book. How sad that space prevented us from finally using them all.

And, most important of all, he had been able to obtain permission to photograph many enormously interesting icons, from Museum and Ecclesiastical archives, as well as from private collections, which had never been either photographed or published before—an exciting coup!

In further meetings with Mr. Vorobyev, Mr. Ginzburg and Mr. Anikst, we discussed the final appearance of the book, the number of pages, the exact color of the cover, the size of the type to be used for the text, and numerous other details. I was also able to read the part of the text which was finished.

When I left Moscow this time, the project was fully under way, a contract had been signed with the Copyright Agency and I was ready to make all the preliminary arrangements for publication of the book in the United States.

This book is a product of the collaboration of a group of extraordinarily talented people to whom I am extremely grateful:

Nicolai A. Vorobyev is a book illustrator and artist in his own right. His works are widely known, internationally as well as in the Soviet Union. He is an avid icon collector and has devoted many years of his life to the study of all aspects of iconography. He writes with a tremendous understanding of the entire subject.

Mikhail A. Anikst, who designed the book, is surely one of the most talented and gifted artists in this field, not only in the Soviet Union, but perhaps in the world. His book designs and graphics have received many prizes and have been displayed at numerous Book Fairs.

George A. Ginzburg is a leader in the Guild of Artists and Photographers in Moscow. For many years he was a script writer and director and responsible for many successful films, both scientific and popular. He has photographed everything from famous people to works of art contained in the superb collections in various Soviet Museums. I think that you will agree that the magnificent fold-out of the Iconostasis on pages 76 to 81 is a masterpiece of photographic art.

It has been a great pleasure and privilege to work with these exceptionally gifted people. I want to thank them, most sincerely, not only for the work which they did, but also for their enormous enthusiasm, as well as their dedication and commitment to the realization of this book—a project which was obviously as interesting and challenging for them as it was for me.

In addition, I wish to thank the members of the Fine Arts Department of the Copyright Agency of the U.S.S.R., who made the publication of this book possible.

L.M.

Manhasset, New York
March, 1986

Contents

How the Icon Came to Russia

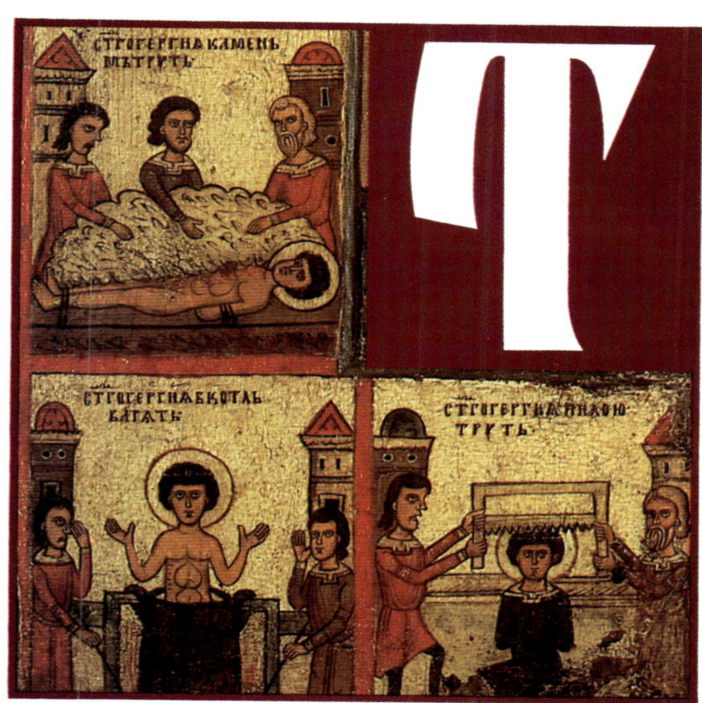

The icon came to Russia late in the tenth century, when Prince Vladimir of Kiev was baptised at Korsun (Chersonesus)—a Greek colony on the Black Sea. Conversion to Christianity gave Russia access to the European culture of the 9th and 10th centuries, and consolidated and developed Russia's ties with Europe's foremost country, Byzantium, which was the preserver of the cultural heritage of Greek and Roman antiquity. A united and powerful state rose around Kiev and Novgorod, with Kiev itself becoming the "Mother of Russian cities".

Prince Vladimir brought back from Chersonesus more than icons, religious books and crosses; he also brought Greek priests, painters and architects for the building and adornment of stone churches which the Prince ordered to be put up on the sites of the pagan shrines he had destroyed.

The foundation of the first stone church of the Holy Virgin was laid in Kiev in the year 989 and was built by Greek craftsmen. The Prince set aside a tenth of his revenue for its upkeep, so that it became known as the Church of the Tithe. The Byzantine architects had gifted pupils. Owing to their skill and experience in building wooden structures they not only excelled in mastering the artistic principles of their tutors, but were able to transform them to suit the tastes and needs of the Russians.

In 1037 Vladimir's son and successor, Yaroslav the Wise, built a huge cathedral in Kiev dedicated to Hagia Sophia, the Holy Wisdom, abundantly adorning its walls with mosaics and frescoes. The Hagia Sophia became the prime Russian cathedral, the coronation church and the burial place of the grand dukes and metropolitans. The first library was founded there, with scribes busily copying spiritual books and chroniclers setting down the events of the time.

1
Winter Landscape with Church in the Town of Suzdal.

The art and learning borrowed from Byzantium gradually assumed more national forms. Native Russian priests and learned monks began to appear, as well as Russian architects and painters. Between the eleventh and thirteenth centuries construction in masonry went on vigorously in many Russian towns. Following Kiev's Cathedral of Hagia Sophia, a cathedral dedicated to the Holy Wisdom was built in Novgorod and Polotsk. Whereas twelfth-century Novgorod developed a rather austere type of single-dome church, Vladimir, the capital city of the Vladimir-Suzdal principality, put up cathedrals of such imposing stateliness, elegant proportions and graceful lines as to stagger the imagination. Among these are the white sandstone Cathedral of the Assumption, the breathtakingly beautiful Church of the Intercession of the Virgin on the river Nerl, and the Cathedral of St. Dmitri, the exterior of which is adorned with rows of stone carvings in the shapes of fanciful plants, beasts and monsters.

The monumental art of construction in stone was not the only art brought to Kiev from Byzantium. Working side by side with Byzantine masters, Russian artists learned the techniques of mosaics, fresco-painting, enameling, and, of course, the art of icon-painting. The word "icon" derives from the Greek word "eikon", meaning "likeness", "image", "representation". An icon-painter, therefore, is an artist "painting images".

Icon-painting originated from Hellenistic portraiture, considerably influenced, incidentally, by the so-called Faiyumic portraits of the 1st to 3rd centuries A.D. discovered in burials of the Faiyum Oasis in Lower Egypt. The Faiyumic portraits were painted with beeswax paints (encaustic) on thin panels of wood. This is the technique of the sixth and seventh century Coptic and Byzantine icons—the oldest that have come down to us, and which unquestionably reveal a stylistic affinity with the Faiyumic portraits. In Byzantium encaustic was replaced by the technique of tempera which uses pigments mixed with egg-yolk.

The first icons to appear on Russian soil were made in Greece and they served as models for Russian icon painters who made

The Virgin of Vladimir is not only the oldest surviving icon brought from Byzantium to Russia, it is also a historical relic associated with many events in Russian history. For the force of feeling it evokes, the work has no equal either in Byzantine or Russian painting.

Mother and Child hold each other in a poignant, tender embrace. There is untold sadness and anguish in the Virgin's eyes. They capture and hold the viewer's attention, for they eloquently express the ageless suffering of mankind.

This work may be boldly ranked with the world's outstanding masterpieces.

2
The Virgin of Vladimir.
First half of 12th century

3
The Apostles Peter and Paul.
Mid-11th century

4
St. Nicholas the Miracle-Worker.
Early 13th century

numerous copies from them, mastering sophisticated icon-painting methods in the process. Elaborated to perfection by Greek masters, the process by which icons were made was taken over by the Russians in its entirety. Yet, while accepting most of the Greek traditions and all the formal aspects of this art, they gradually extricated themselves from the grip of Byzantine ideology. What emerged from under their brush began to acquire their own original national nuances. In the 12th century the chronicles began to mention the name of the gifted Russian icon-painter Alimpi Pechersky.

Icon Painting in Ancient Russia
11th to 13th Centuries

The period from the eleventh to the thirteenth centuries in Kievan Russia saw an unprecedented upsurge of all the arts. This is evidenced not only by architectural monuments, but also by the few surviving mosaics, frescoes, icons, stone sculptures and objects of applied and decorative arts that escaped destruction during the Mongol invasion. The Mongol conquest in the first half of the thirteenth century cut short the development of arts and culture in Old Russia.

The nomad hordes razed many Russian towns and cities to the ground. Moscow, Vladimir, Old Ryazan and Kiev lay in ruins. The invaders spread out among the towns and villages "slashing down people like blades of grass". The alien yoke imposed for many years was no less vicious than the invasion.

Of all the Greek icons imported in great numbers into Kievan Russia, only one has survived—the famous early twelfth-century icon of *The Virgin of Vladimir* (the Vladimir Mother of God). It belongs to the iconographic type designated as *Eleusa* ("tenderness"). Not only is it the oldest surviving icon brought from

5
St. George.
Early 12th century

5

The artist who painted the icon of the Ustyug Annunciation was obviously familiar with the mosaics of the Hagia Sophia Cathedral in Kiev. According to the art historian M.V. Alpatov, it "reminds one of a mosaic transferred onto a large panel."

Byzantium to Russia—it is also a historical relic associated with many events in Russian history. As an iconographic image it had a tremendous influence on Russian painting in subsequent centuries—artists kept copying it until the eighteenth century. In the intervening centuries the icon has been repeatedly subjected to restoration, with the result that nothing but the faces of Mary and the Child remain from the original painting. Nevertheless, for the expressive force of feeling it evokes, the work has no equal either in Byzantine or Russian painting, and may be boldly ranked with the world's outstanding masterpieces. Under the direct influence of this image, which the popular consciousness imbued with the most lofty and virtuous Christian traits of holiness and mercy, a national feminine type—an image of Russian woman—took shape in Russian art. (Plate 2)

After Prince Andrei Bogolyubski, a son of Yaroslav the Wise, moved the venerated Byzantine icon from Kiev to Vladimir, the local cult of the Mother of God began to spread nationwide, so that the icon, since then known as *The Virgin of Vladimir,* came to be regarded as the protective palladium of the Russian state.

In 1395 the icon of the Vladimir Mother of God was transferred to the capital. This happened on the very day when the fearsome Khan Tokhtamysh withdrew his hordes from the walls of Moscow after a long siege. The unexpected deliverance from the foe was attributed to the miracle-working icon, and a special festival, "The Feast of the Purification of the Icon of the Vladimir Mother of God" was established. At the same time the Monastery of the Purification was founded in Moscow. The transfer of the Vladimir icon to the Cathedral of the Assumption in the capital secured for the Cathedral and then for the whole city the name of "The House of the Mother of God".

6
The Ustyug Annunciation.
Second half of 12th century

The earliest work of Old Russian painting that survives from before the Mongol occupations is believed to be the large Novgorodian icon, dated to the eleventh century– *The Apostles Peter and Paul,* now in the Historical-Architectural Museum of Novgorod. The stately posture of the Apostles and the stern manner of execution indicate Byzantine influence, though the images already tend towards the unassuming naturalness characteristic of the Novgorodian icon-painting school. Coming from the Church of St. George in the Yuriev Monastery at Novgorod are two large twelfth-century icons–*St. George* (Plate 5) and *The Ustyug Annunciation* (Plate 6) Both of these icons are now in the Tretyakov Gallery.

The manly individuals whose calm and stern faces look at us from pre-Mongol-period icons, seem full of dignity, ever ready to rise to arms in defense of their motherland. Thus St. George appears on one of the Novgorodian panels as the warrior-saint– an embodiment of strength and soldierly valor.

The icon of *The Ustyug Annunciation* was painted by an artist familiar with the mosaics of the Hagia Sophia Cathedral in Kiev. According to the art historian M.V. Alpatov, it "reminds one of a mosaic transferred onto a large panel."

The icons of the pre-Mongolian period preserved the influence of Byzantine icon-painting both in style and coloring, yet they had already begun to acquire certain qualities distinguishing them from the works of the Greek teachers. These included the fact that they were quite a bit larger in size, a feature uncharacteristic of Byzantine icons

7
The Virgin Orans.
Circa 1224

7

The Creation of an Icon

In Old Russia icon painters were regarded as chosen people. An artist who devoted himself to the art of icon painting had to meet very exacting requirements. When painting an icon he had to follow meticulously certain Church-authorized prototypes, to observe in his private life spiritual purity and bodily cleanliness, to be obedient and humble, to observe all the fasts, to be abstemious and prayerful, and to regularly seek advice from his spiritual father. Nobles and ordinary people alike were expected to treasure and show reverence for good painters. An artist who failed to observe the aforementioned requirements was likely to be banned from icon painting.

The Church admonished the icon painter that his was a lofty and sacred endeavor, it treated him with respect, granted all kinds of privileges, occasionally seeing to it that extraordinary rewards were bestowed on him. For example, the seventeenth-century royal "isographer" Simon Ushakov, was elevated to the nobility.

It was in such an atmosphere of piety that the icon painter's attitude to his art was fostered and cultivated.

Generally speaking, therefore, subjectivity and personal attitudes were uncharacteristic of Old Russian painting. The painter regarded himself as a tool in the hands of God, conveying the epic images molded in the course of centuries in the same impersonal manner as a bard reciting a traditional heroic ballad.

This explains the fact that until the seventeenth century Russian icon painters did not sign their work. Therefore, we do not even know the painters' names, let alone the exact dates of their births and deaths, relation to school or period. Only a very

8
The Virgin Orans.
Detail
Plate 7
Page 19

few names have come down to us. These are of a handful of those painters most venerated by the historians of their time: Alimpi Pechersky, Theophanes the Greek, Andrei Rublev, Daniel Chorny, Dionysius—whose art was deemed worthy of mention in the chronicles and other historical sources. And this was for a tremendously long period of time—from the eleventh through the sixteenth century!

Icon making was a widespread craft in Old Russia. Teams of painter-craftsmen plodded along dusty roads from town to town. They were hired for painting murals in newly-built churches and painting icons for church iconostases. But the main centers for the creation of icons were the workshops of the major monasteries that received commissions from the churches, the Royal Family, boyars and wealthy merchants. Working in these workshops were monks with different specialties. To fulfill an order for a large iconostasis (a four-tier iconostasis consisted of 60 icons) the workshops resorted to collective work. Joint guild manufacture, one of the well-known features of medieval art, was also characteristic of ancient Russian painting.

In church art the surface selected for religious paintings was always the toughest and sturdiest, so as to preserve the image for many centuries to come. In the case of church frescoes, such a surface was a specially treated wall. In the case of the icon it was a primed panel, turned, as it were, into a portion of wall. Such panels were made by special "woodworkers" (carpenters).

The wood used for icon panels was mainly that of the easily worked lime-tree; pine boards were used in Novgorod and Pskov, and fir and larch in the northern areas. From the late eighteenth century the hard and fragrant cypress wood began to be used for icon panels. The carefully selected board, free of knots and well seasoned, was rough-hewed by the carpenter on both sides to the required thickness.

Then a shallow flat rectangular recess *(kovcheg)* with a bevel dip *(luzga)* was worked out on the panel's face at a distance of several centimeters from its edge all along its four sides, using an axe or a special two-handled plane *(teslo)*.

The Virgin of the Sign with Selected Saints.
Detail
Plate 12
Page 24

9
The Prophet Elijah.
First half of 15th century

10
Descent of the Holy Ghost.
15th century

11
The Virgin of the Sign with Selected Saints (Barlaam of Khutyn, John the Almsgiver, Paraskeva Pyatnitsa and Anastasia).
Early 15th century

9

10

11

12

13

One glance at the sturdy relics of Novgorod the Great suffices to fathom the Novgorodian's ideal—a genial fighter, rather uncouth and homely, but shrewd, which is why he won liberty before other people did. He is also more enterprising than his neighbors, which is why he was able to colonize the entire vast Northern territory. His architecture displays the same features he himself possesses—plain but sturdy walls devoid of intrusive, fanciful ornamentation, which he felt was "to no point", bold powerful silhouettes and vigorous piles of masonry. Though not always well conceived, Novgordian architecture is invariably magnificent, strong, stately and overwhelming. This is characteristic, too, of Novgorodian painting, which is colorful, strong, bold and done with a confident hand.

12
The Virgin of the Sign with Selected Saints (the Prophet Elijah, Paraskeva Pyatnitsa, Nicholas the Miracle-Worker, Blaise, Florus and Laurus).
Second quarter of 15th century

13
SS. Florus and Laurus.
Late 15th century

14
The Assembly of the Twelve Apostles.
First half of 15th century

14

17

16

15

"Obeying its rider, a white charger bears down on the dragon in a whirl-wind, as St. George thrusts his spear into its mouth. St. George is represented as the embodiment of goodness and light. This blinding radiance seems like a storm, complete with flashes of lightning, and creating an impression that there is no force in the world capable of barring his swift onslaught."
V. Lazarev

15
St. George and the Dragon.
Late 14th-early 15th century

*16
The Virgin of Mercy.
First half of 16th century

17
SS. Blaise and Spyridon.
Circa 1407

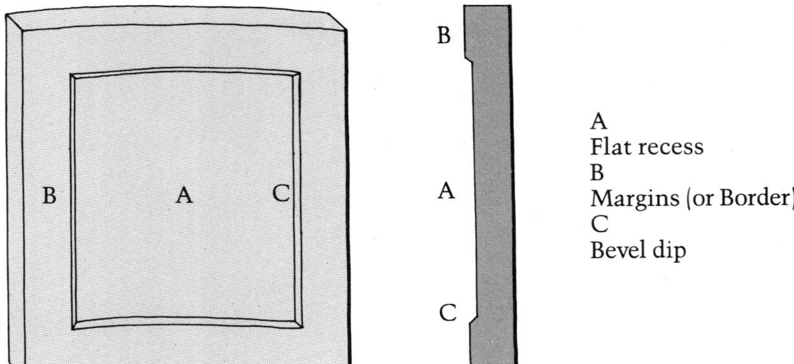

A
Flat recess
B
Margins (or Border)
C
Bevel dip

Whereas in a modern painting it is the frame that creates the illusion of depth, or a kind of "window opening on nature", the borders, or margins of the icon which substitute for the frame, hardly rise above the flat surface of the center piece *(kovcheg)* and are often used for depicting marginal scenes; therefore, they do not produce this effect.

From the second half of the eighteenth century icons no longer had the center-piece recessed, so that the borders were now distinguished from it not by elevation, but by color.

Panels for large icons were made of several planks joined together and reinforced by horizontal wooden slats. Spleens were used to further strengthen the panel.

In the twelfth and thirteenth centuries the slats were fixed to the butts of the planks by means of wooden pegs, or were hammered onto the back of the panel with forged-iron nails.

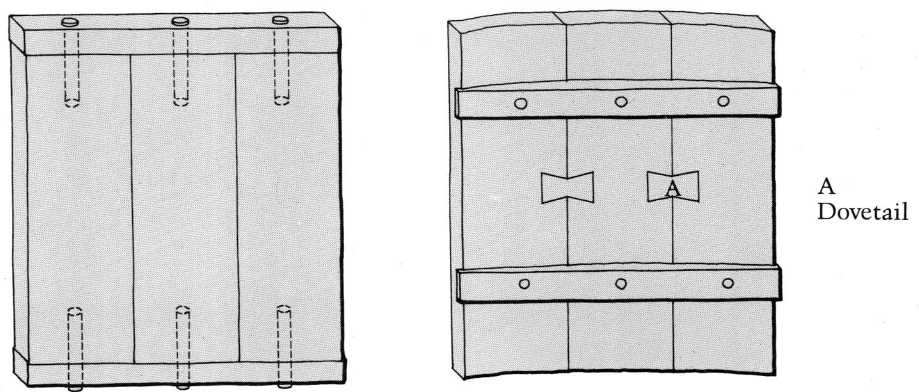

A
Dovetail

Sometimes dovetails were additionally set into the panel for greater strength.

From the end of the fourteenth century the slats were inserted into special grooves cut through nearly the entire width of the joined planks. A small icon panel had only one slat cut into it.

18
St. George with Scenes from His Life.
Early 14th century

18

ПОСЛОВЕ
СУЗАЛЬЦЫ

"What could be more naive, it might seem, than three horsemen, carrying the entire cavalry force on their chargers? Yet just look at the supreme ingenuity by means of which the integral mass of the enemy's cavalry is contained within a single continuous line. The painter has portrayed the tumult of emotions that seized the army, the clash of haphazard and conflicting tempers that resulted in its rout...Only a wizened master of great experience could have created such an integrally accomplished composition as this group of the Suzdalian host...For its cohesion, completeness and balance of forms, it can be ranked with the most superb specimens of Hellenistic art."
M. Alpatov

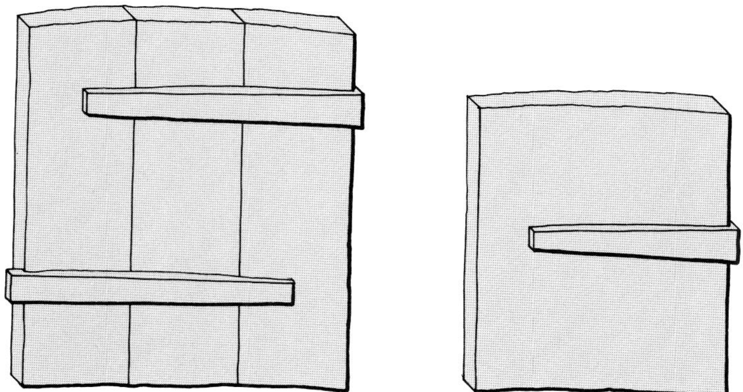

In the seventeenth century the slats were made of oak, low and broad, of intricate shape.

In the eighteenth century the slats were cut into the bottom and top edges of the planks.

Slats were used not for fixation alone; their other purpose was to prevent the warping of the panel.

Therefore, an icon can be dated by the manner in which the slats were applied, by the thickness of the panel (early icons were painted on thin panels) and by whether the center-piece is recessed or not. This however, provided these factors are not contradicted by the style of execution, since old icons were repainted more often than not after a certain period of years.

After the carpenter's job was finished, the icon panel was covered with a gesso ground, but before doing so the master glued strips of flax or hemp canvas onto the panel's upper and lower borders and upon the longitudinal seams if the panel consisted of several planks. This was done in order to protect the gesso ground from cracking and peeling in the most vulnerable places.

19
Battle between the Novgorodians and the Suzdalians.
Circa 1460

20
The Virgin of the Don.
Circa 1390

For centuries *The Virgin of the Don,* an icon attributed to the great Byzantine master Theophanes the Greek, was venerated in Russia next in importance only to the icon of *The Virgin of Vladimir*.

21
The Dormition (on the reverse of The Virgin of the Don).
Circa 1390

The Russian icon is conspicuous for its peculiar combination of an abstract concept coupled with profound emotionality. The Russian icon painter rejected the third dimension and did not apply chiaroscuro, arranging his composition to show not depth but height and subordinating his imagery to the two dimensions of the panel. He regarded the world that he portrayed as a figment of his own pious imagination.

On ancient icons canvas cloth was glued over the entire face of the panel. Beginning with the second half of the eighteenth century, instead of hand-woven canvas, various kinds of machine-made fabrics were used, and in the nineteenth century sometimes ordinary writing paper.

After the panel was covered with canvas, it was "grounded", i.e., coated with a specially prepared priming: a mixture of finely ground chalk or alabaster containing animal glue prepared from the cooking of pieces of hide with the gummy flesh-side retained. Several coats of priming were applied, each being smoothed out with a special metal or wooden spatula *(klepik)*, or simply with the palm of the hand. After all the coats were uniformly dried, the master polished the gesso ground with pumice, continuously wetting it with water, and then finished it off with the stem of the horsetail plant. The durability of the painting, as well as its quality, depended on how well the canvas and priming were applied.

The Old Russian icon painter never sought his images in real life. Of course, some elements of Russian life did find reflection in icon painting, but they were all subordinated to a single style, being secondary, earthly. An icon painter's main inspirational source were the ancient iconographic images that had come to Russia from the dark and hoary past of Byzantium's age-long history, and were held by the Church to be primordeal, prototypal "originals". To many a modern viewer, the icons of the Annunciation, the Nativity, the Crucifixion, are merely ancient pictures with a religious theme. To believers, however, they are historically authentic reflections of real life, and this is why icon painters endeavored to copy the "originals" as accurately as possible.

Just as medieval monk-scribes copied ancient sacred books (prime sources), Russian icon painters of long ago repeated (copied) the ancient iconic "originals". The scholar Pavel Florensky, an authority on Russian icon painting, noted that "the difference between the prototypal icon and a copy from it is about the same as between a description of a newly discovered country and the impressions of a traveller who visited it in accordance with given directions; however historically important were the former, the latter may prove both more complete and more accurate."

22
The Last Judgement.
Third quarter of 15th century

23

24

Russian icon painters through the centuries had to follow the iconographic canon. In order to maintain the canon and preserve it intact, iconographic originals were provided, that is, "guide-books" which indicated the manner in which any particular scene from the life of a saint or an individual scriptural subject ought to be represented. So-called "tracings", copies from ancient icons, were made onto parchment. These tracings were highly valued by the painters, who carefully preserved them, handing them down from generation to generation.

The Church kept a close watch lest icon painters deviate from the ancient tracings, and in the sixteenth to eighteenth centuries numerous originals whose explanatory text was illustrated with drawings, were authorized by special church ordinances.

Every day of the Church Calendar indicates some Christian feast or the feast day of one or another saint.

On the pages of the illustrated manual, shown under the appropriate date, were the contours of the composition pertaining to the feast or a picture of the saint with the designation of his or her facial features, the system of folds on the garments, with slight monochrome coloring to reveal modelling. A brief commentary specified the saint's distinctive marks, such as a moustache or beard, the color of the cloak, garments, or armor.

23
The Descent from the Cross.
Late 15th century

24
The Entombment.
Late 15th century

The Russian icon painter revealed his individuality most strikingly in his understanding of color—the heart and soul of 15th century Russian art. Color provided the Russian icon painter with the means to convey the slightest nuances of emotion.

Thus, the illustrated icon painting manual was a kind of iconographic reference book, a book of rules for the medieval painter. It is only natural that the manuals restricted the artist's creative freedom to a certain degree. However, as the entire history of Old Russian painting demonstrates, within this framework of strict adherence to certain prototypes, there was still the possibility, in the treatment of religious themes and images of the saints, to allow for some personal expression. They managed to invest the basic iconographic sketches with individual ideas and

25
The Nativity of Christ with Selected Saints (Eudocia, John Climacus and Juliana).
First half of 15th century

26
St. Theodore Stratilates with Scenes from His Life.
Late 15th century

"The Novgorodians held strength as their ideal…their beauty is the beauty of strength. Novgorodian painting is similar: vivid colors, strong and bold, brushstrokes laid on with a resolute hand, lines drawn unhesitantly, resolutely and with competence."
I. Grabar

feelings, borrowing both form and imagery from folk art. This turned every icon of one and the same subject into a unique work of art.

As Pavel Florensky justly remarks, "canonic forms in any field of art have always been the touchstone on which nonentities foundered while genuine talent sharpened."

Every painter made his own paints. This was an arduous and protracted chore. The master diligently ground and pulverized the pigments in small wooden or clay dishes after which the finely powdered pigment was mixed with egg-yolk with the addition of *kvas*,* and applied by brush to the gesso-primed panel.

From old *typicons* (painting guides), we learn about the mineral and organic pigments painters used in their work, which of them were imported and which were produced locally. The most costly paint was sky blue, prepared from lapis lazuli, a semi-precious mineral that was imported into Russia via Astrakhan from faraway Bokhara.

Art Historian M.V. Alpatov writes: "The technique of icon painting is not too sophisticated, yet superb in the highest degree. This technique afforded the ancient masters opportunities for creating veritable symphonies in color, by no means inferior to the painting of modern times. The technique permitted the application of many layers, and a diversity of shades and half-tones. It also has advantages over painting in oils. The paints of an icon are capable of retaining all their original brilliance beneath layers of later overpaintings. In most icons we observe the paints in the same condition in which they existed centuries ago."

When commissioned to paint an icon, a skilled painter in an icon-painting workshop would prepare the icon panel himself and then paint it. However, if the workshop received a large order, the principle of division of labor would be applied so that work could be hastened, and the different stages of making the icons would be carried out by "face" painters, "pre-face" painters, draftsmen, calligraphers and gilders, who applied ornamentation to the garments of saints and to the icon's borders. With the development of serial icon making, in the seventeenth and especially the eighteenth century, division of labor among icon painters had become a regular procedure.

*A popular Russian drink made from bread and currants or by pouring warm water over a mixture of rye, barley, or other grain, and allowing it to ferment.

The first to begin was the draftsman, an experienced artist, who drew the chosen subject matter in conformity with an "original" with a brush on the gesso ground.

The arrangement of a multifigured composition on the panel, especially if the panel was large, required great skill, since the drawing applied in black paint to the chalk ground could not be altered during the painting process.

This was not the only method of transferring the drawing onto the panel in Old Russian painting.

When a painter was commissioned to make a copy of a particular icon, he made use of a tracing. Dipping his brush into a special sticky composition, usually thickened garlic or onion juice, he traced the entire composition on the original icon. These outlines could then be "lifted" by pressing a sheet of fine parchment over the surface of the original icon. The parchment bearing a reversed (mirror) pale greyish-green image was then placed onto the gessoed panel, and the master, by stroking it with the palm of the hand produced a direct and accurate imprint on the gesso ground. The juice was then wiped off the original with a damp cloth.

In the seventeenth century the tracing was scratched (engraved) on the gesso ground with a needle, in what was called the "graphic" method.

After the draftsman transferred the drawing onto the gesso ground by any of these methods, the panel was handed over to the gilder.

Ancient icons were gilded with sheets of gold leaf as thin as cigarette paper. The areas to be gilded were smeared with an adhesive paste, after which the master gilder, using a goose feather or a hare's paw, applied thin gold leaf onto the sticky surface and firmly pressed it into place with a special bone spatula. The operation required great care and skill. In the late sixteenth century another less expensive method of gilding appeared—coating with gold reduced to powder and applied as a paint.

In the eighteenth century the gesso was primed before gilding with *poliment*—a special composition consisting of finely pulverized red pigment mixed with aged white of egg containing a dash of *kvas*. The *poliment* layer not only imparted added strength to the gold, but also an attractive reddish hue.

*27
St. Nicetas Giving the Devil a Hiding, with Deesis and Selected Saints.
15th century

29

After the gilding was finished, the head painter began "revealing" the icon's coloristic composition. He built up its main planes of color by filling the contours of the drawing with paint. The "revealing" demonstrated the artist's talent as he worked on the harmonious balance of the entire composition.

Then the icon was handed over to the "pre-face" painter who painted the figures' garments, architectural details, trees, rocks and mountains, pieces of furniture and household utensils and the *pozem* (symbolic designation of the ground); in general everything with the exception of the saints' faces, hands and feet. All the operations were done in strict sequence and had their specific designations: "shadowing"—revealing volume in the darker areas, "whiting"—emphasizing volume in the lightest areas, and, lastly, "illumination"—the final touching up of the entire "pre-face" stage.

From the "pre-face" painter the icon went back to the gilder who now applied ornamentation in gold, the *assist*—the thin gold lines of hatching symbolizing divine light over the garments of the Christ child, over the Saviour's throne, over the representation of the gospels, or the wings of angels.

Whereas in secular art a portraitist would begin painting the head, face, and hands of his sitter, the icon painter painted in the saint's face and hands last of all. The "face" painter's work was regarded in Russian icon painting as the most sensitive, to be entrusted to the best painter available. At first he covered all faces, hands and feet with *sankir*, a layer of flesh priming or shadow tint. An icon's date can be determined by the color of the *sankir*. Ancient Byzantine *sankir* is greyish-blue; that of the fourteenth-fifteenth centuries, green; later it becomes darker, turning tobacco-brown in the second half of the sixteenth century.

*28
The Nativity of the Virgin with Scenes from Her Life.
Late 15th century

29
The Prophets Daniel, David and Solomon.
Circa 1497

After applying the *sankir*, the artist covered the layers of shadow tint with a lighter ochre flesh color, outlining the contours of the faces, hands and feet, accentuating the eyebrows, the eyes, the nose, the lips, the fingers. The flesh color also changed with changes in style: in the fourteenth century it was bright red, becoming darker, browner, in the next century, yet remaining rather soft, before turning all but black in the sixteenth, as the painter harshly accentuated everything "facial" as if with a pen.

The painter then began modelling the image, applying white highlights to the most prominent parts—the forehead, cheeks and bridge of the nose and chin. For this he used liquid flesh color diluted with white and containing ochre. This process bears the name *vochreniye*" ("ochreing"). This stage of subtle gradation in color and soft modelling required the greatest skill, permitting the icon painter to bring the whole image to life, imbuing it with pulsating vitality.

When contemporaries described Andrei Rublev's icons "as if painted with smoke", they not only meant their color tone but the way the paints were applied—in fine, light, transparent layers.

The last thing to be done by the "face" painter was to paint the hair and accent the faces, hands and feet by applying fine white lines and different kinds of highlights ("fresheners", "daubs", "hatchings").

With this ended the role of the "face" painter who passed the panel on to the "calligrapher". This master began adorning the icon: inscribing it with lettering referring to the feast or the saint's name, then drawing the *opush*—a narrow framing line, usually in bright red, occasionally in two colors, along the outer edges of the panel.

When the actual painting was over, the panel was left to stand for a long time to let the paints dry thoroughly, after which the panel was coated with a specially prepared linseed oil varnish—*olifa*. The varnish enhanced the depth and intensity of the colors and protected the paint against moisture.

The varnish-coated icon was kept for a few months with its face to the light to ensure the complete drying of the fine film of varnish.

The icon was now complete. All that remained was to take it to the church for a blessing.

*30
St. Nicholas the Miracle-Worker.
Late 15th century

In the fifteenth century, the Northern areas were under the direct economic, political and cultural influence of the Novgorodian republic. For centuries they preserved excellent specimens of Novgorodian painting as well as panels of other icon-painting schools. These areas also produced their own locally painted icons, amazingly innocent and colorful.

Pagan traditions persisted with particular tenacity and for a particularly long while in Northern Russia, and feeble urbanization caused peasant art to stay pure. It is no wonder therefore that the local icons possess so peculiar a charm, often being amazingly realistic and forceful.

*31
Deesis Tier, Seven Full-Length Figures.
First half of 14th century

*32
The Prophet Elijah in the Desert.
Late 15th-early 16th century

*33
Patria.
Late 15th-early 16th century

31

32

33

The Icon in the Life of the People in Ancient Russia

Hard and cheerless was the life of a peasant in ancient Russia. A sizeable part of his besmoked log hut was taken up by the stove, used not just for heating and cooking, but as a place on which to sleep as well.

The entire household dwelt in the hut in winter–the family as well as the livestock; a cow with her calf, a ewe with her lamb; nor would the sow and her piglets be left out in the cold.

The winters seemed endless and the cold sometimes unbearable. During long sleepless winter nights it was especially depressing and lonesome, so that one was tempted to pour out one's soul to somebody, longing for advice and a little compassion for the woes and bitter fate of life in those days.

Meanwhile, staring out of the "Red Corner"*, the hut's place of honor, were the grave, stern faces of the Saints, darkly glowing in the twinkling flames of the icon-lamps. It was to them–to those silent listeners–that the peasant turned for consolation. He shared with them the needs of his household, told them of the family's joys and sorrows, begged them to protect his loved ones and his livestock, and asked them to intercede for them all before the Lord.

Turning to icons helped man to forget his miserable existence, so full of privations, his aloneness in the hostile world around him. Benevolent, yet at times quite wrathful, the Saints were always there beside him, taking a concerned interest in all his daily affairs.

34
The Prophets Daniel, David and Solomon.
Detail
Plate 29
Page 41

* The "Red Corner" was the corner of the house which caught the first rays of the sun in the morning. This was where the family's icons were grouped.

And this was how it was, from the cradle to the grave...

When a newborn baby was baptized, it was given the name of the saint on whose feast day the baptism ceremony happened to fall. From that moment on and to the end of life, a person acquired a guardian saint he could call his own.

When the time came to choose a trade the patron saints were there to help. Every craft and trade in Old Russia had its heavenly custodians: St. Cosmas and St. Damian extended their favors to healers, blacksmiths and goldsmiths; diggers of wells were assisted by two saints at once–St. Theodore of Tyre and St. Theodore Stratelates. An icon bearing their images was affixed over a newly dug well lest a water-sprite pull down some day-dreaming wife, buckets, yoke, and all...

Want to take up gardening? Ask St. Spiridon, the patron saint of soil fertility, to lend a hand. One of the most popular saints throughout Russian lands was St. George. Not only did he lend power to Russian warriors on the battlefield, but he also looked after plowmen and herdsman. As "Lord of the Wolves" he shielded both human beings and cattle from wolves, just as he repelled serpents from man and domestic animals–another allusion to him as a dragon-slayer.

The cult of St. Nicholas, the Miracle-Worker, "Defender of the Faith" and "Champion of Humankind", was particularly important among the people. To the Russian peasant he stood closest of all the saints. He never minded soiling his garments if need be, and took to heart all the peasant's troubles and worries. He was the protector against fires–a terrible scourge in "wooden" Russia. Ancient legends tell how he miraculously rescued seafarers from drowning at sea, for which he was revered as the patron saint of sailors, fishermen and carpenters.

The Nativity of Christ with Selected Saints.
Detail
Plate 37
Page 47

"Novgorodian and Pskovian icons, with their intelligent and manly images, generalized forms, modest silhouettes, glowing colors–now joyous and ringing, now stern and lucid–with their quite peculiar emotional key, represent one of the highest achievements in Old-Russian painting."
V. Lazarev

35
The Archangel Gabriel.
First half of 15th century

*36
St. Nicholas the Miracle-Worker with Scenes from His Life.
Second half of 16th century

37
The Nativity of Christ with Selected Saints.
Late 15th century

35

36

37

38

Paraskeva Pyatnitsa and Anastasia are the benefactresses of trade. Friday, *pyatnitsa* in Russian, was market day, when people went to bazaars and fairs. Titular churches of Paraskeva Pyatnitsa were, naturally, built in market places. In addition to her main preoccupation, she protected brides and supervised all women's chores, frowning upon women doing any needlework upon a Friday. Those who trespassed ran the risk of being pricked with a distaff or, still worse, being turned into a frog!...

Since he attributed all lucky as well as unlucky events in his life to God's providence, in time of distress man appealed to the

38
Deesis.
13th century

saintly protectors for help: when the hens stopped laying he called on St. Mamas, when the bees stopped swarming he called on St. Zosimus, the miracle-worker of Solovki. To avert fire from his house, he invoked both St. Nicholas and Our Lady of the Burning Bush That Was Not Consumed. To catch a thief he called on St. Theodore of Tyre. If horse thieves ran away with a horse he appealed to Saints Florus and Laurus who were charged with guarding the herds. Icons bearing their images were affixed to the doors of stables for protection against horse spirits which amused themselves by tangling together horses' manes.

Icons protected entrances to houses, yards, streets, lanes and squares against the evil eye. Anyone wishing to pass through a protected area unharmed had to take off his hat and offer a prayer.

The popular mind invested all kinds of religious legends with magical fairy-tale traits. For example, why do the leaves tremble on an aspen tree on a windless day? Because the traitor Judas hanged himself on an aspen, and the poor tree has quivered with horror ever since.

39
SS. Paraskeva Pyatnitsa, Gregory the Theologian, John Chrysostom and Basil the Great.
Early 15th century

39

Carried on the breeze on a sunny fall day are silver spider web threads. These are threads of the Virgin's yarn, and the spinner who glorifies Her will be fortunate in her endeavours. And why doesn't a cuckoo weave her own nest? Because once she did so on the feast day of the Annunciation, when it is a sin to work, not only for people but for all creatures. God punished her, making her roam about and lay eggs in other birds' nests. Thus she misses her young, calling them in vain all through the summer.

In the time when paganism was rife in Russia, each of the elements had its own deity. After conversion to Christianity, certain traits of the pagan gods were transferred to the new saints. The pagan god of thunder and lightning was replaced by the formidable Prophet Elijah. When dark clouds obscured the sun and people heard the rumblings of thunder, they believed it was the Prophet Elijah riding his chariot of fire. He would reward a godly man with a refreshing shower during a dry summer; he would scorch an evil person with fire or beat down his crop with hail. The feast day of Elijah (July 20) was one of the most venerated festivals in Old Russia. Icons depict the Prophet as a stern old man against a fiery-red background, and the icon of *St. Elijah and the Fiery Chariot* is one of the most expressive and colorful in Old-Russian painting.

In the same manner the pagan traits of the spring god Yarilo have been transferred to St. George. Folk tradition holds that on his feast day in spring (April 23), he rides out on a white horse to keep watch over the cattle, let out to pasture after the long winter.

Baales, the pagan "cattle god", has metamorphosed into the Christian St. Blaise of Sebastea, the protector of herds and flocks. On St. Blaise's feast day a jar of milk would be placed in front of his icon, and cows would be driven to the church for a sprinkling with holy water.

The popular calendar and, therefore, the sequence of field work and domestic chores were reckoned according to the saints' feast days, which constituted important landmarks in the workaday life of ordinary folk–the busy times of plowing and sowing, of mowing and harvesting and the periods of hard toil in the fields. When people said: "St. Demetrius of Thessalonica asks for no ferry," it meant that on October 26, the Saint's feast day, the rivers could be expected to freeze up. And March 17, the feast day of St. Alexis, the Man of God, was regarded as the date of the arrival of spring.

40
SS. Paraskeva Pyatnitsa, Gregory the Theologian, John Chrysostom and Basil the Great.
Detail
Plate 39
Page 49

Old Russian painting produced icons named after the lives of the saints. This was a kind of church calendar–a note-book for the believer. There were twelve such icons–one for each month of the year. Depicted on them were miniature representations of the saints and subjects of scriptural feasts arranged in horizontal rows. These pictures clearly showed the days and weeks of the month when different church festivals were celebrated.

Icons, just as books, were used in maintaining family and social records. The family tree, commemoration of ancestors, poor and bumper harvest years, natural calamities, epidemics, and other events were closely associated with icons.

Icons were treated with great reverence. They were handed down from generation to generation and were witnesses to all the family's joys and sorrows. In the popular mind a saint and his or her image were quite inseparable, the icon representing, as it were, the saint's materialized image.

The demand for icons was very great indeed. Markets in the sixteenth to eighteenth centuries had special icon sections, where anyone could buy an icon of his favorite saint. Yet the words "buy" and "sell" were not used. It was thought that to say "I bought an icon" was tantamount to saying "I bought a saint". So it was said instead: "An icon was exchanged for money."

Having penetrated into the remotest parts of ancient Russia, icons became an indispensible attribute of every home in town and countryside alike. They were placed on a shelf in the "Red Corner", which was adorned with embroidered homespun towels; suspended from the shelves were hangings with portraits of saints embroidered with colored silk, silver and gold thread and mother-of-pearl. The seat beneath the icons was a place of honor reserved for the most esteemed guests.

Well-to-do people covered their icons with silver and gold *oklads* or *rizas*. *Oklad* refers to embellishments applied to the icon on halos, *tzatas*, garments or borders, whereas a *riza* covered almost the entire icon with the exception of the faces, hands and feet. Various kinds of metals, pearls, filigree, enamel, embroidery, silver, gold, precious or semi-precious stones, or any combination of these elements, were used on both *oklads* and *rizas*. In some cases, *oklads* or *rizas* were made for an icon long after it was painted. Therefore, an 18th century icon could have a *riza* made for it in the 19th century.

*41
Four-Part Icon: The Descent into Limbo, The Trinity, Three Selected Saints, and The Nativity of Christ.
Second half of 15th century

Not only people enjoyed saintly protection; every village and town had its own heavenly patrons. For example, Novgorod was regarded as a city of St. Sophia, after whom the Novgorodian cathedral church was named; Pskov, a city of the Holy Trinity with its Cathedral of The Trinity, and Moscow, with its Cathedral of the Assumption, was the city of the Mother of God.

Church festivals brightened up the monotony of Old Russia's everyday life. Most of them celebrated the chief scriptural events, or were dedicated to individual saints or "miracle-working" icons. The most important took place during the Christmas season and the weeks preceding Shrovetide and Easter.

Many of these festivals had already existed among the ancient Slavs and were adjusted by the church to corresponding dates in the Christian calendar, thereby perpetuating traits of pagan rites.

At Shrovetide, for instance, the merry crowd burned an effigy. Then they set wheels on fire and rolled them down a hillside. These rites symbolized the burning away of winter and a welcome to spring.

To the Russian of long ago, the icon was more than a mere object of religious veneration. It brought out the capacity to appreciate beauty and perfection and instilled a profound confidence in truth and love reigning supreme in some kingdom beyond the clouds.

The Trinity.
Detail
Plate 55
Page 63

In the fourteenth century, Moscow became the political, religious, and cultural center of the Grand Principality of Moscovy. The Moscow icon-painting school gradually developed into an independent trend in Old-Russian art, becoming, with the passage of time, the dominant one. Its evolution, from the end of the fourteenth through the fifteenth and sixteenth centuries, was profoundly influenced by the works of the great Russian painter Andrei Rublev.

42
SS. Boris and Gleb.
Mid-14th century

43
DIONYSIUS
The Virgin Hodegetria.
1502

44
Christ in Majesty.
Second half of 15th century

42

43

44

45

46

47

48

45
SS. Boris and Gleb with Scenes from Their Lives.
Second half of 15th century

46, 47, 48
Marginal Scenes of the Icon of SS. Boris and Gleb.

49

50

51

*49
The Virgin of Yaroslavl.
Second half of 15th century

*50
Paraskeva Pyatnitsa with Scenes from Her Life.
16th century

51
DIONYSIUS AND DISCIPLES
The Descent into Limbo.
1502

The Pictorial Language of the Russian Icon

The icon, to those who cannot read, is what scripture means to the learned. This medieval dictum is quite true of the people of Old Russia.

Even if unable to read or write, a believer very well understood the language of Old-Russian art. Being thoroughly familiar with religious subjects, he knew why, in one case, a saint held a key in his hand, in another—a book, knew the meaning of an architectural detail or tree in a composition, and why it was depicted on the left rather than on the right.

By gazing at frescoes and icons in church, the illiterate Russian "read" the gospels. Instead of the language of the printed word he read the language of colors. For centuries this language was cultivated and enriched.

Since many a spectator today is unfamiliar with religious subjects, the icon painters' pictorial language is alien and strange to him. Christian art is basically a symbolic art. In order to learn to "read" an icon it is essential to know the most characteristic features of this conventional language.

For example, featured in the icon of the Nativity are three wise men from the East—the Magi hastening to bring gifts and pay homage to the newborn Jesus. They personify three human ages: youth, maturity and old age. Underlying such personification was a definite symbolic idea, namely, that all mankind, the young and the old, should embrace the Christian doctrine.

The gifts of the Magi (gold, frankincense and myrrh) also have a dual symbolic meaning. A gift of gold in homage to a newborn prince was a customary one in many countries, including Russia; frankincense was brought in homage to his divinity; myrrh, used in the East for embalming the dead before burial, here symbolized a foreshadowing of his death.

"The exceptional artistic gifts of Theophanes illuminated the art of Novgorod with such a brilliant flame that its reflections could be felt in Russia for many years to come." I. Grabar

52
School of **THEOPHANES THE GREEK**
The Transfiguration.
Circa 1403

54
ANDREI RUBLEV
The Apostle Paul.
Circa 1410

Also used in icon painting was the symbolism of gesture. If an icon represents a saint with his hand touching his cheek—it is a sign of sorrow, if the saint is touching the tips of his fingers to his lips, it means silence.

All sacred and venerated personages are represented on icons with a golden, or in some cases colored, radiance around or above the head. This shining radiance is called a *nimbus*, which in Latin means "cloud" or "mist". A *nimbus* is a symbol of divinity and sacredness, and it takes different forms. Christ is depicted with a cross *nimbus*, the Virgin, Angels and Saints—with a circular one, the circle being a symbol of everlasting life and eternity.

A *nimbus* is a general attribute, but there are also strictly individual ones. For instance, the four evangelists, Matthew, Mark, Luke and John, saintly authors of the four canonic gospels, are identified by an angel, a lion, an ox and an eagle respectively. Other attributes of the evangelists are a scroll or book.

The icon painter had his own shorthand system. When he wished to stress where something was occurring, he used a whole system of what might be called "conventional signs" to immediately make it clear to the spectator where this or that event was taking place. Thus, a blue segment with gold specks or stars in the icon's upper portion indicated the star-studded heavenly orb. One, two or three trees, could signify a thick forest or, depending on the subject, the garden of paradise. Stepped-up rocks indicated an entire mountain range; a turret—a palace; a crenelated fortress wall—a city.

If the saint was shown sitting on a throne or a chair, with a table, burning lamp or some other domestic article in front of him, it meant that the scene was taking place in an interior. To make things absolutely clear, the painter might place architectural "wings"—two turrets with a cloth draped between them—on the sides, or he would depict a wall in the background with a tree growing behind it. However, if the tree was shown in front of the wall, this meant that the action was taking place outdoors.

In distinction from the ascetic Byzantine image of Christ, the face of Rublev's Saviour expresses not only heavenly severity, but also love; not only divine majesty, but also earthly compassion for sinful and helpless man.

53
ANDREI RUBLEV
The Saviour.
Circa 1410

"Rublev's colors sing. Those of Novgorodian icons ring out. Their strident colors are attractive, but they do not have the tender, elegant coloring of the Moscow school—which eloquently expressed the most delicate spiritual sensations."
M. Alpatov

When seasons of the year, the elements, manifestations and forces of nature had to be depicted, the artist again resorted to the language of symbols and allegories. A maiden enthroned and wearing a royal crown and mantle symbolized Spring, a winged nude youth blowing a trumpet—the Wind; a young shepherd sitting on a hill personified Mount Sinai; old men and youths, more seldom women, holding slim-throated amphoras with water flowing from them personified streams and rivers.

Allegories of this kind, essentially harking back to the pagan deities of rivers, mountains and the elements, were carried on into medieval painting through Hellenistic art.

The colors used in icon painting also had a dual meaning—natural and symbolic.

Russian icon painters knew about the symbolic significance of colors from the ancient Greek theory of color, according to which red recalled the blood of martyrs, blue symbolized the heavens and contemplation; green was a sign of youth and life; white, the "divine color", stood for purity, and black was an embodiment of death and the darkness of hell.

Color symbolism was widely used in Russian icon painting. When used on an icon, a definite color became an "identification mark" of certain objects. For example, the Virgin was always portrayed in a dark cherry-red cloak; Apostle Paul—in a bright carmine one, Apostle Peter is depicted in an ochre cloak; St. George and St. Paraskeva Pyatnitsa in red cloaks—signs of martyrdom. The austere Prophet Elijah is usually depicted against a fiery-red background, a color symbolizing the eternal flames of hell.

Scarlet red was always a favorite color in Russian culture. It is not accidental that the second meaning of the Russian word *krasny*, for "red", means "beautiful".

Gold in an icon is the symbol of divine energy, associated with the "never setting sun". As distinguished from paint, it depicts nothing, for it is immaterial. Events depicted against a gold background assume a special meaning that places them outside the concept of time; gold is used to indicate only that which is related to divine energy.

55
ANDREI RUBLEV
The Trinity.
Circa 1411

56, 57
ANDREI RUBLEV
The Trinity.
Detail
Plate 55
Page 63

55

58

In addition to symbols, Russian icon painting made use of a host of attributes. According to the gospels, Jesus charged Peter, "The Prince of the Apostles", with being his bishop on earth and entrusted the keys to the Christian Church to him. When presented on icons, St. Peter is shown holding in his hand a gold key—his attribute.

Apostle Paul is one of the pillars of Christian theology, and the icon painter puts a book into his hands.

An icon of St. Nicholas of Mozhaisk (the city which, according to tradition, St. Nicholas the Miracle-Worker defended against foes) shows the saint with the model of a church held in one hand and a drawn sword in the other.

The magnanimous healers Saints Cosmas and Damian hold boxes with medicines in their hands. Prelates are depicted with closed gospels, prophets—with scrolls, martyrs—with crosses, angels—the divine messengers—with pilgrims' staffs as an allusion to their mediatory role between God and people. The wavy

58
DIONYSIUS
The Virgin Hodegetria.
1482

Dionysius was considered reverently immediately after Theophanes the Greek and Andrei Rublev—artists regarded as the most accomplished icon painters in Old Russia. His work left an imprint on all Muscovite painting.

hair of angels is tied with ribbons symbolizing "hearing" which points to omniscience. An archangel holds in his hand a "flawless mirror". When God's message arrives, the archangel's "hearing" is alerted and he visualizes the Lord's command in the mirror. This is how theologians explained these attributes.

One of the greatest conventions of Old-Russian icon painting is the representation of events as they unfold in time. In a single composition, the painter combines various episodes of one and the same story, showing what happened prior to the central event, and what was going to take place afterwards.

59

59
PROCHORUS OF GORODETS
The Last Supper.
1405

By way of example, let us take the composition of the fifteenth-century Novgorodian icon of *The Nativity* in the Tretyakov Gallery, Moscow. (Plate 25)

According to the gospels, Mary and Joseph, her husband, set out for Bethlehem from Nazareth. Arriving towards nightfall, they found no room in the inn, but were lucky to find a nearby cave which served as a stable, and where Mary, who felt the moment of delivery approaching, gave birth to the Son of God. His cradle was a manger and a sheaf of straw served as a mattress.

Night fell. Shepherds driving their flocks home met an angel who announced the birth of the wonderful Child. They heard throngs of angels singing in praise of Him.

A new star lit up the sky; so bright it was that it could be seen throughout the world, and the Magi in the East saw it, too. They took gifts and went to pay homage to the newborn Prince, following the star that led them right to the cave.

The town of Bethlehem is situated on a hill and in all the compositions of the Nativity we see mountains and rocks. The scene of Christ's birth is depicted in the center of the icon. The Virgin is reclining on a cloth spread over the stony earth. Beyond, against the dark background of the cave, one can see a manger with the swaddled child, and the heads of an ox and an ass, the most docile of creatures.

Shining above the mountain is the star of Bethlehem, whose blue rays reach into the cave.

On the left stand two singing angels and below them, hastening from the East to pay homage to the newborn Christ are three Magi bearing gifts. To the right of the cave, on the other slope of the mountain, another angel is announcing the good tidings to a shepherd. The shepherd is beneath him, blowing a horn to spread the good news throughout the area.

The panel's lower part contains another two scenes unconnected in time either with each other or with the central episode. On the left we see Joseph sitting in deep thought, and an old man in shepherd's robes in front of him. According to one interpretation, this is the Devil. Having assumed a respectable appearance he whispers evil thoughts into Joseph's ear, hoping to arouse suspicions about his wife's fidelity.

On the right two midwives are making preparations for bathing the newborn; one holds in her lap the unswaddled baby (the child is depicted twice in the same composition), the other is pouring water out of a jar into a font.

60
DIONYSIUS' Workshop.
St. Cyril of Byelozersk with Scenes from His Life.
Late 15th century

60

62

63

The Old-Russian master's conceptions of space and time are equally abstract. He compresses long periods of time into an instant, just as he shrivels the boundless vastness of the Earth into a single small area of pictorial surface. Without giving it a thought, he brings all the personages of the story into close proximity, though, according to the theme, they must all be in quite different places. Joseph, who went into the mountains in search of the calming effect on his soul, the midwives busy around the font, the Magi hastening to Bethlehem from the other end of the world, the shepherd blowing his horn, angels bringing good tidings and singing–all of them are arranged on the icon side by side in three horizontal and three vertical rows, so that they can be seen easily at a single glance.

Thus, represented simultaneously in one icon and one composition are all the main events of the Nativity cycle.

61
DIONYSIUS
The Crucifixion.
1500

62
The Dormition.
Circa 1497

63
DIONYSIUS' Workshop
In Thee Rejoiceth.
Early 16th century

In order to understand the content of the Nativity icon and realize the role of every personage, it must be "read" part by part, though from the purely aesthetic point of view, the impression is that of wonderful integrity. In addition, one may note other specific features of the icon-painting language on this icon.

For example, according to common sense, the bathing scene should take place indoors, as indicated by the font. Two angels personify throngs of angels, one shepherd–several. The blue segment with three diverging rays–the night sky with the Star of Bethlehem, and the few fanciful bushes–thickets of orange trees covering the mountain.

Space and volume hardly exist for the icon painter. In addition to direct perspective, to which we are accustomed, whereby objects decrease in size with distance, he uses that special so-called "reverse perspective" in which objects are presented as seen by the personages in the icon, from their respective points of view, rather than by a spectator looking at the panel.

Reverse perspective is a conventional system for conveying the three-dimensional characteristics of the real world on a flat surface. An icon's spatial depth is always rather shallow, with differently spaced figures and objects seemingly brought into close proximity. The icon's conventional lack of depth may be compared to a sculpted bas-relief which fails to produce the illusion of spatial depth, but merely hints at it. But in sculpture this device is wholly dependent on the nature of the material. The shallowness of icons is a peculiar device, conducive to setting the world of the icon apart from ordinary realistic conceptions. The icons' lack of the illusion of depth is a distinctive feature of Old-Russian painting.

Apart from recognized masters, a great number of highly skilled icon-painting craftsmen, who catered mainly to ordinary folk, were active in Old Russia. The fruitful bonds that always existed between professional and folk art added to the overall high standards of Russian painting. One should not forget, however, that the creative endeavor of the best painters and architects in ancient Russia was in the service of religion and it would be wrong, when looking at the Russian icon, to disregard its relation to the church.

The Russian icon is as amazing for the intensity of each individual color as the finest antique murals. However, while the few known specimens of these murals go no further than the beauty of an isolated color, the icon paintings achieve wondrous beauty by blending several colors—a fusion attained not by transition from color to color, but by their bold contrasts.

64
The Dormition.
Detail.
Plate 62
Page 71

The Russian Church
The Iconostasis

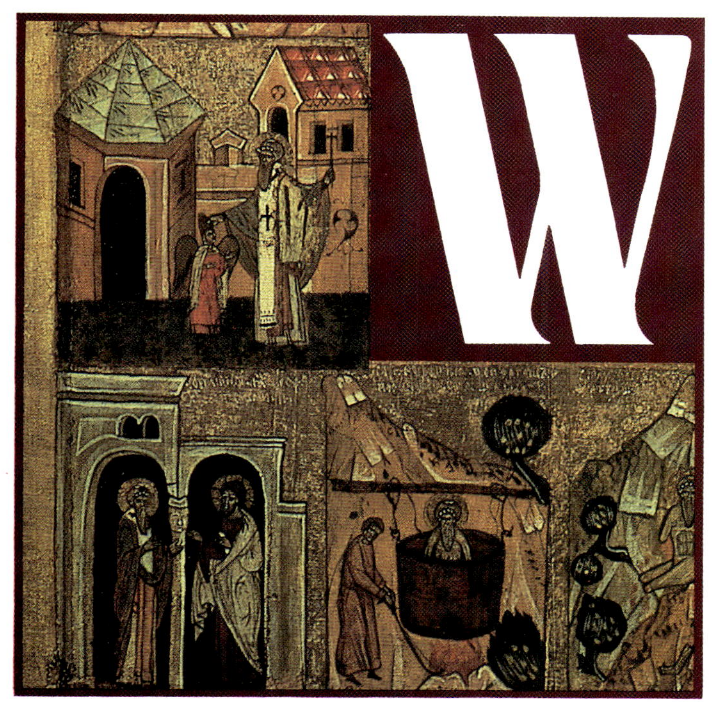

With the conversion of Kievan Russia to Christianity, many fine churches began to be built on the sites of former pagan shrines. Through the ages the church became a fixture in the Russian landscape, blending harmoniously with its surroundings, whether standing on a river bank, or rising on a hillock amidst a copse of white-barked birches.

Even in the modern city, among the high-rises built of concrete, metal and glass, a church, far from being obscured, stands out and commands attention, attracting the eye with the unassuming elegance and graceful simplicity of its architectural forms. How uniquely beautiful is the silhouette of the Moscow Kremlin, with the domes of its numerous palaces, churches and cathedrals! The gold onion-shaped cupolas of white stone churches, the Ivan-the-Great Bell-tower lifting its shining gold dome high above Moscow, and, outside the Kremlin walls, the Church of St. Basil the Blessed rising in Red Square have an exotic, fairy-tale beauty. All these are remarkable and unforgettable architectural monuments. On the banks of the Moskva river stands the amazing Novo-Devichi convent, whose mighty fortress walls were built more than four centuries ago.

No less impressively blending with the natural landscape is the Kolomenskoye village complex, with its proudly soaring Church of the Ascension. It was built as a thanksgiving gesture by Grand Prince Basil III in 1532 for the birth of his long-awaited son and heir, the future Tsar Ivan IV.

Moscow is far from the only city that can boast of fine church architecture. Standing in austere beauty are the magnificent churches and cathedrals of Novgorod, Pskov, Suzdal, Vladimir, Vologda and many other towns and cities.

65
In Thee Rejoiceth.
Detail.
Plate 63
Page 71

66

In the North of Russia, rising above the vast expanses of lakes and islands are wooden churches of modest, quiet parishes as well as imposing monasteries—witnesses to the selfless endeavor of the Russians who brought life to these harsh severe lands.

The church architecture of Russia is profoundly national, without any analogy in West-European architecture.

If, even today, an old church building fills us with admiration for its technical perfection, originality of form and amazing affinity with its surroundings, one can easily imagine how strongly it was bound to affect and move the deeply devout Russian of old, whose entire life was closely linked with the church! In all kinds of weather, hail or shine, men, women and children of every age, all clad in their Sunday best, went to church in answer to the ringing of church bells.

66
The Monastery of the Intercession at Suzdal.

They brought to "God's House" all their joys and sorrows. Here they hoped to obtain succor and advice from their patron saints and to receive absolution for their sins.

In the light spacious church, which smelled of pinewood and incense, a person felt as unconfined as in the fields, as calm and quiet as near a forest lake. The entire atmosphere, enhanced by the sparkling candles and twinkling icon-lamps, the glitter of gold and silver icon rizas, the richly adorned robes of the priests, the choir's heartfelt singing, created a tremendously emotional and festive mood.

A special place in the sumptuous decoration of a Russian church goes to its main adornment—the Iconostasis.

Not very high in the small wooden churches, but becoming a solid wall often reaching as high as the vaults in the large stone cathedrals, the iconostasis is an integral part of the grandiose ensemble making up a Russian church.

The iconostasis had a special symbolic significance within the interior of a church, partitioning off the nave, the space intended for the congregation—the visible, earthly, material world, as it were, from the sanctuary—the invisible, heavenly, spiritual world. The saints depicted on the icons of the iconostasis are, to those living on the earth, the visible witnesses of that invisible heavenly world, concealed from the eyes of believers behind the iconostasis screen. They are the windows through which the congregation may see that world and worship it.

Frozen in postures of reverence, the immobile prophets, apostles and saints gathered around Christ seem to be interceding together with the prayerful congregation before the Heavenly Judge.

The hierarchic order of saints on an iconostasis is arranged in tiers around the figure of Christ according to a specific order.

For a better understanding of the symbolic meaning of a five-tier iconostasis let us begin from the upper to the bottom tier.

The topmost tier, bearing the name "Patriarchal", personifies the Old-Testament pre-Christian church. Occupying the center of this tier is an icon of God the Father, with images of the Old-Testament patriarchs (Adam, Abel, Seth, Noah, Enoch, Abraham and others) on both sides of Him.

70

71

72

81

82

83

The iconostasis is contrived so as to be taken in at one glance. Hence its strict compositional arrangement. Gravitating towards its accentuated central axis are its two flanks. In it the horizontal and vertical sections are presented in subtly conceived rhythmic combinations, every element integrating into a well-arranged composite whole subordinated to tectonic principles. It required a simple clear-cut composition, and conventionalized line, even for the many Festival icons.

68

69

*68-78
Festive Tier from the Iconostasis of the Cathedral of the Assumption at Sviyazhsk. Mid-16th century

68 **The Annunciation.**

69 **The Nativity of Christ.**

70 **Presentation of Christ in the Temple.**

71 **The Baptism of Christ.**

72 **The Raising of Lazarus.**

73 **Entry into Jerusalem.**

74 **The Transfiguration.**

75 **The Trinity.**

76 **The Incredulity of Thomas.**

77 **The Descent of the Holy Ghost.**

78 **The Raising of the Cross.**

*79-88
Deesis Tier from the Iconostasis of the Cathedral of the Assumption at Sviyazhsk. Mid-16th century

79 **St. John Chrysostom.**

80 **St. Basil the Great.**

81 **The Apostle Peter.**

82 **The Archangel Michael.**

83 **The Virgin.**

84 **Christ in Majesty.**

85 **St. John the Baptist.**

86 **The Archangel Gabriel.**

87 **The Apostle Paul.**

88 **St. Nicholas the Miracle-Worker.**

79

80

*67
17th-Century Iconostasis.
Ecclesiastical Academy, St. Sergius Monastery of The Trinity, Zagorsk
(A three-tier Iconostasis)

The next is the "Prophets" tier. In the center, beneath the icon of God the Father, is a half-length image of the Virgin of the Sign with arms raised in prayer, bearing on her breast a medallion of Christ Emmanuel with His hands extended in a similar way. This iconographic symbol of the Virgin embodies the "Holy Virgin containing in Her bosom the image of the Son born to Her", which, in turn, personifies the birth of the New-Testament Christian Church. On both sides of the Virgin hang icons presenting the prophets, witnesses of Christ's coming into the world.

The "Festive" tier is dedicated to the main events of Christ's earthly life and usually includes the following subjects: The Annunciation, The Nativity of Christ, The Presentation in the Temple, The Baptism (the Epiphany), The Raising of Lazarus, The Transfiguration, The Entry into Jerusalem, The Crucifixion, The Descent into Limbo, The Ascension, The Descent of the Holy Ghost, and The Assumption.

This tier is called "Festive" because the events represented here have been linked by the Church to certain dates celebrated as festivals.

Below the "Festive" tier is the "Deesis" tier. "Deesis" is a Greek word meaning "prayer".

Situated in the center of this tier is an icon of the Saviour Enthroned, with the Virgin on his right and John the Baptist on his left. These three personages are joined by the Archangels Michael and Gabriel, the Apostles Peter and Paul, and Prelates—Fathers of the Church and Ecumenical Teachers. The Deesis tier also frequently depicts St. George and St. Demetrios of Solonika, the heavenly soldier-saints.

The aesthetic principle of an iconostasis is based on a solemn and prayerful rhythm, the main role in this religious structure being played by the Deesis tier, the chief tier of the iconostasis. Its icons are also the largest.

The last, bottom tier of an iconostasis is called "Local". It contains, on both sides of the Royal Doors leading to the altar, icons of the Saviour and the Mother of God, icons of the saint or saints to whom the church is consecrated and the icons of the most venerated local saints.

St. Hypatius of Gangra.
Detail
Plate 89
Page 85

The icon-painting school of Tver stood out among the central Russian principalities in the thirteenth to the sixteenth centuries for its distinctive stylistic features: flowing lines, a rather whitish color scheme and a very original palette.

89
St. Hypatius of Gangra with Scenes from His Life.
First half of 15th century

*90
Apostle Paul from a Deesis Tier.
Second half of 15th century

*91
The Nativity of the Virgin.
16th century

73

74

75

84

85

76

77

78

86

87

88

89

90

91

The Royal Doors were painted by an icon painter, their finial icon depicting the Annunciation–the appearance of Archangel Gabriel before the Virgin to announce the good tidings that she was to give birth to the Son of God, the future Saviour. Depicted on the panels of the Doors were the four evangelists: St. Matthew, St. Mark, St. Luke and St. John, who brought Christ's word to the world, thereby opening the doors of Heaven to mankind.

In the fourteenth century the doors to the altar sometimes depicted the Eucharist, a subject that later was placed above them. The Eucharist is the communion of the apostles, Christ's disciples, by partaking of bread and wine, symbolizing the body and blood of Christ.

Placed in the center of the Deesis tier, the image of Christ serves as the ideological core of the iconostasis, which governs the choice and arrangement of the subjects into a unified harmonious whole.

The Prophets are those who predicted the coming of Christ into the world. The Festivals are the main episodes of His earthly life, the Eucharist is a reminder of His redeeming sacrifice, the Prelates are those who officiate at the mystery of the Eucharist, Deacons and Angels are the visible and invisible ministers in the mystery, the Evangelists are heralds of the Christian doctrine.

The iconostasis is intended to be seen at a glance, hence its austere design. It has a clear-cut central axis towards which movement is directed from both sides; the horizontal and vertical subdivisions are presented in subtle and well-thought-out rhythmical combinations. It forms a harmonious whole subordinated to the principles of tectonics. Thus even the multifigured festive icons have a simplicity and clarity of composition, lest they should fail to be discerned above the Deesis tier. The iconostasis has a precise pictorial language which was preserved through the centuries.

In all probability the first iconostases appeared in Russia and began their development in forested areas where small wooden churches were built, which had no space for murals. Without the latter a church was bound to lose beauty and splendor. Something had to compensate for the absence of mural paintings and this was the iconostasis.

This is also confirmed by the fact that transferred with amazing consistency to the iconostasis were all the main themes of mural painting, and the distribution in tiers inevitably followed the same laws of symbolism as prevailed in the frescoes.

The iconostasis developed gradually. In the twelfth century only one Deesis icon was placed over the central doors of the altar screen: Christ in the center with the Mother of God on his right and John the Baptist on his left. Gradually the number of icons increased, making up a whole tier, then another was added above it.

The first four-tier iconostases appeared in Novgorod early in the fifteenth century. They were not large in size because the churches themselves were small. In the magnificent cathedrals that went up in the Grand Ducal capital of Moscow, the iconostases increased in size, gradually assuming monumental proportions.

Old Russian painting produced icons named after the Lives of the Saints. This was a kind of church calendar–a note-book for illiterate people. There were twelve such icons–one for each month of the year. Depicted on them were miniature representations of the saints and subjects of scriptural feasts arranged in horizontal rows. These pictures clearly showed the days and weeks of the month when different church festivals were celebrated.

*92
Lives of the Saints for November.
16th century

In 1405, the great painters Theophanes the Greek, Prochorus of Gorodets and Andrei Rublev, created a grandiose iconostasis in the Kremlin's Cathedral of the Annunciation, including in it a full-figure Deesis tier which was more than two meters high. The height of the Deesis tier painted by Andrei Rublev for the Cathedral of the Assumption in Vladimir was more than three meters.

The seventeenth century, with its penchant for decorativeness, saw the appearance of huge eight-tier iconostases. Vertical columns in prominent relief and horizontal struts between the tiers and the icons were covered with fine gilded carving. Succulent clusters of grapes and vine leaves entwined the entire iconostasis and Royal Doors from top to bottom, their glitter eclipsing the painting.

This kind of altar screen foreshadowed the baroque magnificence of the eighteenth-century iconostases. Despite all kinds of changes in styles of painting and in the richness of decoration, the iconostasis remains the pinnacle of Russian icon painting. This magnificent piece of decorative art was created by the joint efforts of many talented artists: painters, architects, wood carvers and gilders. The iconostasis became a school and training ground for Old-Russian masters, enhancing their realization that the icon may be perceived in two ways: at close range, revealing all the minute narrative details, and from a distance, which allowed the viewer to take in its overall composition, rhythms and proportions.

To the Russian, the church was more than a place of worship. From early childhood on, it familiarized him intimately with different kinds of art—painting, sculpture, music and ornamentation. The Church not only molded his moral principles, but his aesthetic taste as well.

93
Lives of the Saints.
Detail
Plate 92
Page 87

The Russian Icon

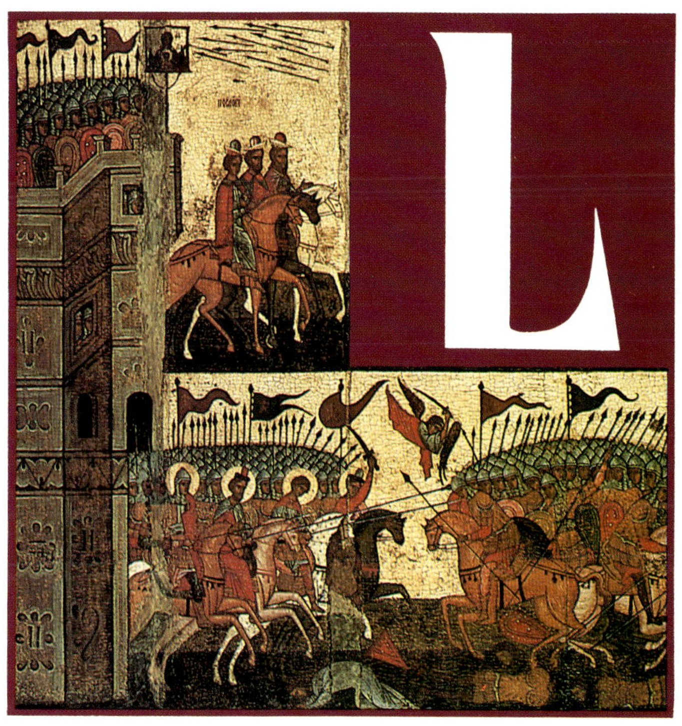

Lord Novgorod and Pskov, its "younger brother" were the only Russian cities to remain unmolested during the terrible years of the Mongolian invasions. They were protected by the dense forests and marshes that proved impassable to the hordes of Batu Khan. But the thirteenth century was a "dark age" even for these free northern republics. Building in stone was virtually at a standstill. Trade and cultural ties with southern Russia and Byzantium were disrupted. No masters arrived from Constantinople; the influx of Greek icons ceased. Such isolation prepared the ground for the penetration of national motifs and popular forms into the art of Novgorod. As icon painters gradually departed from the austere Byzantine traditions, Novgorodian icons became more vigorous, albeit more primitive . At the same time, departure from the "lofty style" of the eleventh and twelfth centuries marked the beginning of explorations along new lines, which led Novgorodian painting to the shining summits it reached in the late fourteenth and the fifteenth century.

The revival of Novgorodian art and Russian culture in general was boosted tremendously by the great victory on the battlefield of Kulikovo in 1380. Vigorous construction began in Novgorod. Trading and craft guilds sponsored the building of numerous stone and wooden churches in their respective streets and boroughs; this, in turn, encouraged the development of pictorial arts, icon painting first of all.

Icons were in great demand. Painters were often commissioned to depict the most venerated Novgorodian saints, patrons of agriculture, protectors of flocks and herds and of commerce, such as the Prophet Elijah, St. George, St. Blaise, Sts. Florus and Laurus, St. Nicholas, St. Paraskeva Pyatnitsa, and St. Anastasia. The practical Novgorodian, instead of commissioning several icons bearing the images of his patron saints, ordered just one, in which

94
Cathedral of the Intercession–Church of St. Basil the Blessed.
16th century

all his protectors and patrons appeared together, usually standing in a row. Such icons with "selected saints" became quite popular in Novgorod.

In Novgorodian fifteenth-century painting the Byzantium-inspired ascetic and austere images of the saints underwent gradual transformation, becoming more "humane" and acquiring a new emotional tenor. Thus, Byzantine and pre-Mongol Russian icon painters depicted St. George as a Triumphator upon a prancing charger after his slaying of the Dragon. They emphasized his mighty physique and severity–"...his gaze instilled fear in all who looked at him." In Novgorodian icon painting the image of St. George shed its solemnity and stateliness, becoming more graceful, full of youthful charm, knightly valor and fairy-tale sparkle.

The Virgin of the Sign with Selected Saints.
Detail
Plate 12
Page 24

Outstanding among the Novgorodian icons of *St. George and the Dragon* is a late fourteenth-early fifteenth century panel depicting the soldier-saint against a crimson-red background (Russian Museum, Leningrad). The eminent art historian V. Lazarev describes this icon as follows: "Obeying its rider, a white charger bears down on the dragon in a whirlwind, as St. George thrusts his spear into its mouth. He is represented as an embodiment of goodness and light. This blinding radiance seems like a storm, complete with flashes of lightning, and creating an impression that there is no force in the world capable of barring the swift onslaught of this intrepid warrior." (Plate 15)

A classical example of Novgorodian art at its height is the fifteenth century icon depicting *The Battle Between the Men of Novgorod and the Men of Suzdal* (in the Museum of History and Architecture, Novgorod), one of the first paintings in the historical genre in Russia. It commemorates a twelfth-century episode in the history of Novgorod, rather than a biblical theme. The icon painter describes a miracle worked by the icon of *The Virgin of the Sign,* venerated as the city's protectress. According to ancient tradition, when the Novgorodians were besieged by superior Suzdalian forces led by Prince Andrei Bogolyubski, they took the miracle-working icon from the church and placed it on the fortress wall, facing the enemy army. When the arrows of the Suzdalians hit the icon, it turned its face from them, toward the city, at the same time taking the bright light which emanated from it away from the Suzdalians, leaving them in utter darkness and confusion. Taking advantage of this situation, the Novgorodians, who saw everything clearly from the light of the icon, were able to capture and kill the Suzdalians. (Plate 19)

The icon of *The Battle between the Men of Novgorod and the Men of Suzdal* is an example of a complex composition which is at the same time clear and lucid. It is divided horizontally into three parts in which the events connected with Novgorod's miraculous deliverance unfold from top to bottom. Particularly expressive, as if carved from a single block of stone, is the group of Suzdalian cavalry in the last, bottom row. The eminent art historian M. Alpatov, commenting on the skill the Novgorodian artist displayed in the composition of this episode, writes: "What could be more naive, it might seem, than three horsemen, carrying the entire cavalry force on their chargers? Yet just look at the supreme ingenuity by means of which the integral mass of the enemy's cavalry is contained within a single continuous line. The painter has portrayed the tumult of emotions that seized the army, the clash of haphazard and conflicting tempers that resulted in its rout...Only a wizened master of great experience could have created such an integrally accomplished composition as this group of the Suzdalian host...For its cohesion, completeness and balance of forms, it can be ranked with the most superb specimens of Hellenistic art."

The fourteenth century saw the emergence in Novgorod of special biographical icons. They existed also in Byzantium, but it was only in Slavonic countries, and particularly in Russia, that they became widespread. The center piece of such icons usually depicted a saint, while different scenes from his or her life were presented in rectangular paintings in the margins.

The early fourteenth-century icon of *St. George with Scenes from His Life* (now in the Russian Museum, Leningrad), executed in a bright, decorative manner, colorfully and gracefully narrates the warrior-saint's life, presenting him as a person of great moral fortitude and spirituality. Many of the marginal scenes depict the terrible tortures to which the saint was subjected. In distinction from Western painters who presented similar subjects with realistic frankness, the Russian icon painter evaded the portrayal of excessively gory details. His task was to convey "not the image of pain , but the ideal of the beauty of suffering" for faith and justice. (Plate 18)

There are very few ancient icons with representations of St. Nicetas beating the Devil. The fifteenth-century icon of *St. Nicetas giving a Hiding to the Devil, with a Deesis Tier and Selected Saints* (in a private collection) is one of the earliest in Russian icon painting. The icon's center-piece shows St. Nicetas beating the Devil. A legend tells us that when he was incarcerated by his cruel father the Emperor Maximilian, the Devil appeared to him in the guise of an angel. But the Saint recognized the Devil and, having removed the shackles from his feet, began beating him. The idea of the victory of good over evil is presented here by the use of colors. Bright, intensive colors–red, blue, green and orange–surround the dark space of the prison, defeating the hellish darkness with a glow of bright, festive pigments. The official church treated the image of St. Nicetas as a holy martyr and valiant soldier. In the popular mind he was a protector against the forces of darkness, against diabolic delusions. Small crosses, amulets and other objects bearing his image were widespread in Russia. (Plate 27)

Novgorodian painting of the fifteenth century is often called the "Golden Age" in the history of Russian art. Never before nor after did the national artistic language reach such expressive force, such terseness and severe beauty. "The Novgorodians held strength as their ideal," wrote the art historian Igor Grabar, "their beauty is the beauty of strength. Novgorodian painting is similar: vivid colors, strong and bold, brushstrokes laid on with a resolute hand, lines drawn unhesitantly, resolutely and competence."

Theophanes the Greek

A special place in Novgorodian and Pskovian painting goes to the work of Theophanes the Greek, one of the greatest artists of the Middle Ages. He arrived in Novgorod from Byzantium in the 1370's, at the height of his creative powers. His talent unfolded to the full in Russia where Theophanes lived for about thirty years and where he died at an advanced age, supposedly in 1405. At any rate, this is the last date under which the chronicles mention his name in connection with a Grand Ducal commission.

Contemporaries were full of the highest praise for his genius, and applied to him the most exhalted epithets: "this wonderful and illustrious person," "an accomplished philosopher, excellent book illustrator and by far the best among the icon painters." Surviving is a letter by the Muscovite writer Epiphanius the Wise who knew the Greek master well. "At the time of my sojourn in Moscow," wrote Epiphanius in 1413, "living there was the famous sage and most accomplished philosopher Theophanes, born a Greek." And further: "No one ever saw him look at models

School of Theophanes the Greek.
The Transfiguration.
Detail
Plate 52
Page 58

as is done by certain of our icon painters who, doubting everything, make constant use of them, looking hither and thither—not so much working their paints as compelling themselves to look at a model. But he, it would seem, painted on his own, all the time moving about, conversing with visitors, and while he discussed everything other-worldly and spiritual, with his outward gaze he saw that spiritual beauty."

Very few works by Theophanes have come down to us. If the attribution of the monumental murals in the Church of the Transfiguration on Ilyin Street in Novgorod, which he painted in 1378, is unquestionable, the authorship of panel paintings, with the exception of the icons of the Deesis tier of the Cathedral of the Annunciation in Moscow's Kremlin, is still a subject of controversy. This is also true of the late fourteenth century *Virgin of the Don,* (Plate 20) with a *Dormition* (Plate 21) on the reverse side, a masterpiece of Old-Russian painting. Yet, as V. Lazarev justly maintains: "This is a work of exceptional artistic merit, irrespective of whether we attribute it to Theophanes or his school."

The history of *The Virgin of the Don* is wrapped in legend. According to tradition, it was presented by the Don Cossacks to Grand Duke Dimitry of Moscow on the eve of the Battle of Kulikovo. The Duke's campaign was waged "under the sign of the Virgin". He scheduled the rallying of his troops at Kolomna on the Feast of the Assumption, and the battle itself on the Feast of the Nativity of the Virgin. Victory was attributed to the presence on the battlefield of the Virgin's icon, which personified the Virgin Mary Herself. In honor of that great victory the icon was awarded the same title as the victorious Grand Prince, who went down in history as Dimitry of the Don, (Dimitry Donskoy) so that to this day it is known as *The Virgin of the Don.*

It has been presumed that Theophanes was commissioned to paint the icon of *The Virgin of the Don* in commemoration of the icon that accompanied Prince Dimitry in his campaign and perished during the battle. For centuries the icon painted by the great Byzantine master was venerated in Russia next to the icon of *The Virgin of Vladimir.* In the sixteenth century it was at Kolomna in the Ascension Cathedral, where Ivan the Terrible prayed in front of it before setting out on his Kazan campaign. In 1591 Boris Godunov, in connection with the attack of the Crimean Khan Kazy-Girey against Moscow, brought the miracle-working icon to the capital. Upon the unexpected retreat of the Tatar cavalry from the Kremlin walls, the miraculous deliverance of Moscow from the invasion was ascribed to the icon and Tsar Feodor founded the Don Monastery, in which the icon of *The Virgin of the Don* was installed as its principal holy object.

No less important is the reverse of the panel, bearing the icon of *The Dormition of the Virgin*. The apostles in this scene hardly resemble austere Greek prelates and have none of the Byzantine aristocratism about them. They are shown gathered around the Virgin's bier, unanimous in their profound personal sorrow. Above the Virgin's body and the figures of the apostles rises the shining figure of Christ with the soul of the Virgin in his hands, invisible to those present. Earthly people, they are not destined to learn the mystery of Mary's everlasting life. Christ alone knows the mystery, for he belongs to two worlds simultaneously, the divine and the human.

Coming also from Theophanes' workshop is one of the most monumental paintings of the late fourteenth-early fifteenth century, the style of which combines Greek and Russian traits—the icon of *The Transfiguration*. (Plate 52)

It shows how Jesus, with the apostles Peter, Jacob and John went up to Mount Tabor, situated not far from Nazareth, for prayer. While praying on the mountain peak, Christ's face was suddenly transformed. His face began shining like that of the sun and his garments turned white as snow. The painter depicts everything bathed in the rays of glory: the transfigured Saviour, the Prophet Elijah on the left, and Moses on the right. Beneath, scattered about the foot of the mountain are the very expressive figures of the Apostles, blinded by the rays of Mount Tabor's light. In the mid-portion of the icon there are scenes depicting the events that preceded and followed the main episode—on the left Christ and the apostles ascending Mount Tabor, and on the right—their descent.

"The exceptional artistic gift of Theophanes," wrote art historian I. Grabar, "illuminated the art of Novgorod with such brilliant flames, that its reflections could be felt in Russia for many years to come."

After the victory on the battlefield of Kulikovo, Moscow, the Grand Ducal capital, became the hub of Old Russia's political and cultural life.

Four-Part Icon.
Detail
Plate 41
Page 53

It was at the beginning of the 1390s that Theophanes arrived in the capital, where he at once gained prominence among Moscow's icon painters. Together with Prochorus of Gorodets and the monk Andrei Rublev he was commissioned to paint icons for the Cathedral of the Annunciation in Moscow's Kremlin. The Byzantine artist was the team's head master. He executed the personages of the Deesis tier of the iconostasis with his own hand. He was the first in Russia bold enough to paint icons on panels more than two meters high and one meter wide.

The iconostasis of the Annunciation Cathedral with its full-length figures of the Deesis tier set a classical standard for Russian multi-tier iconostases which in subsequent centuries became widespread in Old-Russian art. The saints depicted by Theophanes on the Deesis icons are austere and tense and are markedly individual.

The talented Byzantine master, with his profoundly dramatic images and his interest in man's innermost world, had a great influence on Old-Russian painting.

The Pskovian School and Northern Icons

Until the middle of the fourteenth century Pskov was subordinated to Novgorod. Later, upon gaining complete independence, it turned into a political center on a par with Novgorod and developed its own culture to suit its own tastes and needs. Despite its territorial proximity to its great neighbor, Pskovian icon painting is distinguished for its own unique and original traits.

Pskovian painting follows a more archaic manner. The figures on its panels are more static, presented frontally with a stressed simplicity of contours; there is an abundance of gold assist on the garments, the dramatically saturated color scheme is dominated by deep-green and brown-red pigments, characteristic of the Pskovian palette. Many of these pigments were of mineral origin, obtained locally, and did not, therefore, occur in the works of other painting schools.

Pskovian icon painters gave little heed to traditional iconographic types and unhesitatingly introduced all the changes they deemed necessary. They worked without tracings, drawing the preliminary outline in black paint directly on the gesso ground; their brushwork was broad and sketchy, and though they could not match Novgorodian painters for fineness of execution, their panels were superior in expressive force and naturalness in representing human sorrow and suffering.

There is no doubt that Pskovian, just as Novgorodian painters, were familiar with the works of Theophanes the Greek, had known and seen icons painted by him and were bound to fall under the spell of the Byzantine master's genius.

Though the Novgorodian and Pskovian schools existed quite independently of each other, there is, nevertheless, much that is common betwen them. First of all, simplicity and expressiveness and, mainly, the strong influence of popular crafts and arts. Hence the deep originality of Novgorodian and Pskovian art. "Novgorodian and Pskovian icons," wrote V. Lazarev, "with their intelligent and manly images, generalized forms, modest silhouettes, glowing colors, now joyous and ringing, now stern and lucid, with their quite peculiar emotional key, represent one of the highest achievements of Old-Russian painting."

In the fifteenth century, the Northern areas were under the direct economic, political and cultural influence of the Novgorodian republic. For centuries they preserved excellent specimens of Novgorodian painting as well as panels of other icon-painting schools. These areas also produced their own, locally painted icons, amazingly innocent and colorful. In the North, among the boundless expanses of forests and lakes, away from large human settlements, pagan traditions survived and peasant crafts retained their purity. On a summer evening, and especially through the long drawn out winters, peasants would engage in the painting of icons, distaffs, birch-bark boxes and shaft bows in their huts. Their handicrafts were closely connected with household needs and the nature surrounding them.

No other field of Old-Russian painting was linked so immediately with everyday life as Northern icons, hence their underivative and inimitable qualities. Defining the latter, V. Lazarev writes: "These, first of all, were their images, which were those of common people depicted with a primitive realism.

They had an artless design and execution. In vain one looks for any special refinement of sentiment, yet their profound sincerity is always captivating. They possess a naive and guileless simple-heartedness; the inscriptions often are in a local dialect, and the ornamentation is a direct link with objects of applied art. The faces of the saints reflect the influence of local peasant types. The coloring loses the vividness and resounding quality of the Novgorodian palette. It is dominated by subdued, somewhat turbid tones which are in tune with the interiors of wooden churches and the soft hues of the Northern landscape."

Andrei Rublev
The Saviour.
Detail
Plate 53
Page 60

Andrei Rublev

Very little is known about the life of this famous painter. The chronicles hardly mention anything but the towns where Rublev worked and the churches for which he painted icons and frescoes. He was probably born between 1360 and 1370, and died circa 1430. The fifteenth century *Tale of the Sacred Icon Painters* relates that Andrei Rublev and his teacher and life-long friend Daniel Chorny were monks of the St. Sergius Monastery of the Trinity which they left towards the end of their lives for the Andronikov Monastery of the Saviour, where they died.

In 1405 Rublev was already quite well known. Otherwise he would not have been summoned to work on the murals of the Annunciation Cathedral in the Moscow Kremlin together with the famous Theophanes the Greek and Prochorus of Gorodets. Working with the Byzantine master influenced Rublev considerably and contributed to the further development of his talent.

In 1408 Andrei Rublev and Daniel Chorny were commissioned to restore the murals in one of the most venerated churches in Russia–the Assumption Cathedral at Vladimir.

In addition to the work on the murals he painted the icons for the iconostasis together with a team of artists. All his work shows a keen interest in human personality and man's spiritual world. These aspects of the artist's talent are especially evident in the images of St. Peter and St. Paul in the Deesis tier of the Assumption Cathedral.

Rublev and Chorny returned from Vladimir to the St. Sergius Monastery of the Trinity where, during the first and second decades of the fifteenth century Rublev created some of the best of his works: the *Zvenigorod Tier* and his *Old-Testament Trinity.*

Only three icons survive from the *Zvenigorod Tier:* the half-length figures of the Saviour, the Archangel Michael and Apostle Paul. They were discovered in 1918 in a shed near the Ascension Cathedral at Zvenigorod and were far from intact. In distinction from the ascetic Byzantine image of Christ, the face of Rublev's Saviour expresses not only heavenly severity, but also love; not only divine majesty, but also earthly compassion for sinful and helpless man. (Plates 53, 54)

According to the *Tale of the Sacred Icon Painters*, Nikon, the Dean of the St. Sergius Monastery of the Trinity who succeeded St. Sergius of Radonezh, "commanded the monk Andrei Rublev to paint a Trinity icon in praise of his Father, Saint Sergius the Miracle-Worker." A biography of St. Sergius tells us he built the Trinity Cathedral "so that by gazing at the Holy Trinity the terror of this world's hateful strife would be overcome." Andrei Rublev, his pupil and adherent to his philosophy, painted his famous icon of *The Trinity* in commemoration of his teacher.

According to the Christian doctrine, the one God is manifested in three beings: God the Father, the creator of heaven and earth and all that is visible and invisible; God the Son, Jesus Christ, who assumed a human aspect and descended from heaven to earth for the sake of redeeming mankind; and God the Holy Ghost, imparting life to all that exists (represented in icons by the image of a white dove in a radiant nimbus). The Deity, being a union of three persons, has no definite image, but at times, according to Christian tradition, appears to people in the guise of an image comprehensible to man. And so He appeared to Abraham in the guise of three angels. Abraham guessed that the three strangers represented the three beings of the Trinity. Filled with joy, he invited them to take seats in the shade of an oak, commanded his wife Sarah to bake unleavened loaves with the best flour, and bade a servant to kill a fattened calf. This story is told in Genesis, the first book of the Old Testament, and this is why Rublev's composition is called *The Old-Testament Trinity.*

Before Rublev, Byzantine and Old-Russian painters never went beyond the simple illustration of the biblical story in their icons, a treatment whereby the idea of a tri-une deity never found truly imaginative expression. Rublev abandoned extraneous personages and narrative details. The only tribute to the iconographic tradition remaining of the ancient legend are the oak of Mamre, the chambers, the table, and the pilgrim staffs in the hands of the angels.

Three golden-haired, golden-winged angels are seated at a low table; their heads are inclined, their gaze expresses sorrow, their lips are sealed. The angel in the middle points questioningly at the chalice with sacrificial calf—the icon's substantial and compositional center, symbolizing Christ's redeeming sacrifice. The gesture of the angel on the left, full of solemn grief, confirms, as it were, the inevitability of the sacrifice, while the angel sitting on the right slowly lowers his hand, as if concurring with him. The figures of the angels are inscribed into a circle—the symbol of eternity. The whole composition is permeated with a subtle rhythm which governs the arrangement of the figures and their flowing outlines, the inclined heads of the angels and the conforming silhouettes of the hill, the chambers and the tree.

The tranquil postures, the smooth rhythm of the lines, the lucid colors—all engender a sensation of peace, calm and harmony. This is exactly what has always been lacking on Earth. Thus, the subject matter of *The Trinity* transcends the merely theological ideal to become universal. In this composition, Rublev embodied the aspiration of his fellow men to live in peace and unity, observing the laws of amity and justice. Rublev's genius as an artist lies in his ability to reveal the complex and profound philosophical content of *The Trinity* through his use of paint, rhythm and color. (Plates 55, 56, 57)

In one way or another the real world of the nature surrounding them left its mark on the painting of Old-Russian masters. The bright colors of Novgorodian icons reflect the flaming summer sunsets of the North. The color range of Rublev's *Trinity* is attuned to the hues of central Russian nature in summer: blue cornflowers, pale-green oats, the golden fields of wheat. M. Alpatov remarks in this connection: "Rublev's colors sing. Those of Novgorodian icons ring out. Their strident colors are attractive, but they are unfamiliar with the tender, elegant coloring of the Moscow school—an expression of most delicate spiritual sensations."

In 1425 Andrei Rublev, together with Daniel Chorny and a large team of painters, created the icons for the iconostasis of the Trinity Cathedral in the Monastery of the Trinity.

His contemporaries described him as a quiet and humble person "of superlative wisdom" and "perfect virtue". As a monk of the Andronikov Monastery he lived in strict seclusion. He painted icons, showed little interest in anything earthly, elevating his mind and thoughts "towards immaterial and divine light", and on festive days and weekdays free from painting, he seated himself in front of ancient icons for long periods of time, admiring and enjoying them. These qualities of the mind and heart left a deep, pure and enlightened imprint on all his art.

Andrei Rublev died at an advanced age, after having painted the Cathedral of The Saviour in the Andronikov Monastery. Unfortunately only two insignificant details of floral ornaments survive from these murals. This was the cloister in which "Andrei the icon painter" found his last resting place.

After Rublev's death his icons were highly valued; news of their loss was recorded in the chronicles as events of great importance. The Church now required that icon painters should "paint icons from ancient prototypes as Greek painters did them, and as Andrei Rublev did them".

All subsequent generations of icon painters in Russia were under the immediate influence of Rublev's work. The best works of the fifteenth century evidence loyalty to his aesthetic ideals. The work of this great master fully combined the classical Byzantine heritage adopted by Russia with a profoundly national perception.

Today the Andronikov Monastery is the Andrei Rublev Museum of Old-Russian Art. It was opened to the public in 1960 on the 600th birth anniversary of the greatest of Russian painters.

Dionysius

Construction on a grandiose scale went on in Moscow in the late fifteenth and early sixteenth centuries. Most of the newly built cathedrals were adorned with rich, sumptuous paintings.

The best architects, armorers, icon painters, stone, wood and metal carvers were assembled in the Moscow Kremlin. This period of the growth of culture and the arts coincided with the activities of the famous icon painter Dionysius.

DIONYSIUS' Workshop
St. Cyril of Byelozerak.
Detail
Plate 60
Page 69

Born between 1430 and 1440, Dionysius died in 1508. Together with his sons Vladimir and Theodosius he painted frescoes and a great many icons for iconostases for churches and cathedrals both in Moscow (Cathedral of the Assumption in Moscow's Kremlin) and in the Russian North (the Cyril Byelozersk and Ferapontov Monasteries). Wherever he worked, fame followed. He was acclaimed as a "clever and most elegant" painter. He may have lacked the passionate intensity of Theophanes, and the serene transcendence of Rublev, but his work is marked by a special refinement. The figures are deliberately elongated, with handsome and beautiful faces, yet they are not very expressive and are very much alike, as twin brothers. His compositions are always harmonious, measured and stately. The artist strove for elegance of outline, refinement of posture and gesture.

The entire coloristic and representational system of the painter's icons and frescoes reminds one that those chosen by the heavens are void of human passions, an impression further enhanced by the lucid hues he used which were of an almost water-color transparency. His art has something in common with music, and this is equally true of his icons and of the uniquely beautiful and expressive murals in the Nativity Cathedral of the Ferapontov Monastery (the only surviving fifteenth century fresco cycle).

Only a few icons painted by the famous master survive. One of them is an icon of *The Crucifixion* from the iconostasis of the St. Paul Monastery at Obnorsk, painted in 1500. Rising high above Calvary and the walls of Jerusalem is a tall black cross with the crucified Jesus. His slightly bent figure, with arms outstretched, seems to be soaring in space. The silent, frozen figures of those standing at the foot of the cross, Christ's face, calm and without a trace of suffering, turn the scene of the terrible execution and bereavement into a solemn, timeless act, where there is no place for ordinary human sentiments. The clear-cut figures, and the rhythm of the garments' folds produce a sensation of inner rigidity. The glow of the pure pigments–green, pink, gold, crimson and sky-blue against the background of the snow-white walls–hints that the days of grief and sorrow will give way to the joy of the Resurrection. (Plate 61)

Several biographical icons created in Dionysius' workshop survive. V. Lazarev notes that "Biographical icons were painted in Russia in the twelfth, the thirteenth and the fourteenth centuries. But only in Dionysius' time did they acquire the aesthetic refinement which turned them into outstanding works of Old-Russian painting."

95

The icon of *St. Cyril of Byelozersk with Scenes from His Life* was painted at the end of the fifteenth century for the Assumption Cathedral of the St. Cyril Monastery in Byelozersk. The center-piece portrays St. Cyril, the founder of the Monastery which in the fourteenth century became a center of education and culture and a frontier fortress of the Muscovite state in the North. The marginal scenes unfold a detailed story of the Saint's life. (Plate 60)

Historians mention Dionysius with reverence immediately after the names of Theophanes the Greek and Andrei Rublev—artists regarded as the most accomplished icon painters in Old Russia. His work left an imprint on all Muscovite painting. But towards the middle of the sixteenth century the aesthetic principles of Dionysius had notably waned. The coloristic pattern of the icons changed, losing the transparency and polychromy of Dionysius' palette; the figures become more thick-set, even squat. Also lost is the elegance of postures, nor do we observe any

*95
SS. Procopius and John of Ustyug. Silver Oklad
17th century

96
Three-Leaf Folding Icon (without central portion).
17th century

97
PROCOPIUS CHIRIN
St. John the Baptist—Angel of the Desert.
17th century

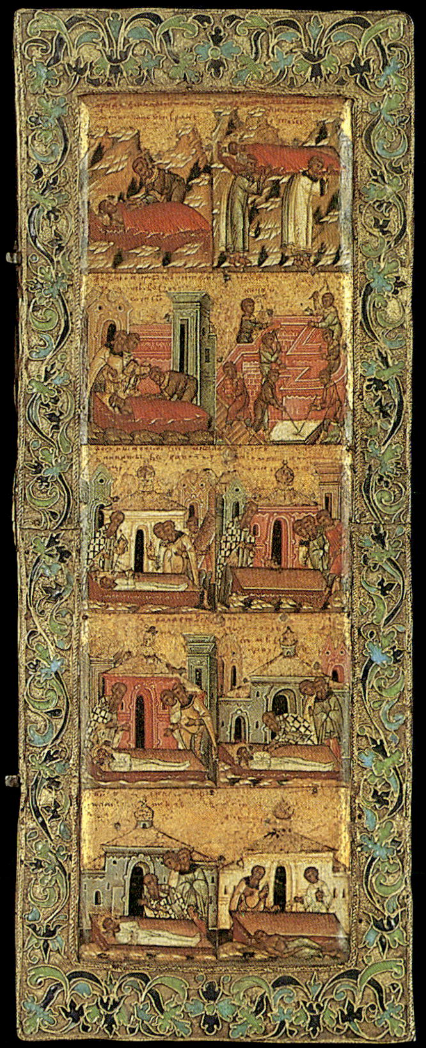

96

97

longer those perfectly balanced compositions. There appears a striving for narrativeness, for linear decorativeness, stylization of forms—evidence that the secular principle was gaining ground in icon painting. Gold literally invades the painting. Masters are no longer content with gold paint, they replace it with the genuine product. Fine gold leaf with repoussé ornamentation is applied to the halos surrounding the saints' heads, and later on to the background. But whereas, according to V. Lazarev, "in the fourteenth and fifteenth centuries balance is still preserved between the painted image and the oklads, since the latter bear a fine, light ornament in repoussé, well agreeing with the plane of the iconic panel;" in the sixteenth and, especially the seventeenth century this equilibrium is upset. The painting is obscured in the glitter of gold and heavy rizas adorned with multicolored enamels and gems, covering almost all the pictorial surface of an icon.

Three-leaf folding Icon
Detail
Plate 96
Page 105

All these new qualities of Russian icon painting found a most vivid manifestation in the icons of the so-called Stroganov school.

The Stroganov School

The Vision of Sexton Tarasius.
Detail
Plate 101
Page 111

The Stroganovs, a wealthy family of Russian industrialists and merchants, were famous for generations as great patrons of the arts. At their seat in the northern town of Solvychegodsk they maintained icon-painting workshops, employing first-rate masters. This is how in the period from the sixteenth to the eighteenth centuries an interesting development took place in Russian icon painting, known, conditionally, under the name of "The Stroganov School." Conditionally, because most of the icons known under this name came out of the royal workshops in Moscow. But since they were stylistically identical with those of the Stroganov painters, they became united also by name.

The Stroganov school has its own distinguishing features. Small in size, the icons have very broad margins, usually covered by precious *oklads*. The painting is marked by a miniaturized style whereby the painters carefully render the facial features and details of garments on small figures sometimes only 1 to 2 centimeters high.

Another peculiarity of this school's icons is the abundance of gold. Garments, foliage, blades of grass—all are shimmering with gold assist. The paints, applied in elegant combinations, are as bright as colored enamels.

*98
The Virgin of the Sign with Scenes from Her Life.
Second half of 17th century

Stroganov icon painters treated some of their subjects as fairy-tale scenes. The garments of the personages present a comprehensive study of Russian costumes from the late-sixteenth to the early-seventeenth century. These icons, intended to be admired at close range, like jewelry, have always been popular with collectors, becoming quite rare as early as the seventeenth century.

98

**Icon Painting in the 17th Century
Simon Ushakov**

In his *Vernicle* icon Ushakov endeavored to represent an earthly man with the imprint of suffering on his face, rather than the formidable Deity of the twelfth century, or the exhalted Saviour of the fourteenth or fifteenth century.

The Armory was founded in the Moscow Kremlin at the beginning of the sixteenth century. By the seventeenth century it was the hub of artistic activities in Russia. In order to fulfill royal commissions, the Armory enlisted the aid of icon painters from different towns that had their own painting schools: Vladimir, Kostroma, Yaroslavl and Nizhni Novgorod.

The Armory's icon painters were called "Royal Isographers". Outstanding among them in the late sixteenth and early seventeenth centuries were Procopius Chirin and Istomin Slavin. However, the leading figure, who headed the Armory for forty years, was Simon Ushakov.

Ushakov was born in 1625 and died in 1668. He was widely educated and became very versatile. He painted icons and portraits, made engravings, drew geographical maps, embroidered banners, engaged in the art of fortification and theorized over new trends in Russian painting. In his treatise *An Address to Connoisseurs of Icon Painting* he compares painting with a mirror reflecting the "images of diverse objects." This opinion crystallized Ushakov's views on the art of icon painting, views which determined its development to the middle of the eighteenth century.

The stately, attractive, colorful and at the same time naturalistic painting of the "Ushakov school" was considerably influenced by West European art. This influence resulted from the broad dissemination in Russia of West European engravings, the so-called "foreign sheets", which became quite a vogue in the households of royalty and the boyars.

There appeared a new "foreign" style in icon painting, which abandoned the strict iconographic patterns in favor of more natural forms, lighter, rounder faces instead of the lean ascetic visages depicted on ancient icons.

There are quite a number of icons extant bearing Ushakov's signature. On icons with multifigured compositions created together with other masters, he painted the faces only. Contemporaries believed Ushakov had no equal in the rendering of faces.

The seventeenth-century icon of the *Vernicle (Saviour Not Painted by Hand)* in the collection of the Tretyakov Gallery is just one of the *Saviours* by Ushakov. The name of the icon is explained by the ancient legend of the third or fourth century A.D. It relates how the image of Jesus was impressed upon the veil offered to him by St. Veronica on the road to Calvary. (Plate 99)

99
SIMON USHAKOV
The Vernicle (The Saviour Not Painted by Hand).
17th century

100
The Last Judgement.
17th century

101
The Vision of Sexton Tarasius.
Late 17th-early 18th century

102

103

In his *Vernicle* icon Ushakov endeavored to represent an earthly man with the imprint of suffering on his face, rather than the formidable Deity of the twelfth century, or the exhalted Saviour of the fourteenth-fifteenth centuries.

The artist seems to have molded the face by the gradual buildup of many layers, a technique allowing him to convey the mental state of the image. Igor Grabar wrote that "such faces were never painted in Moscow, either during his lifetime, or after." This striving to impart corporeality to his personages can be felt in all the icons by Ushakov, his disciples and followers.

In the first half of the seventeenth century there appear in Russian icon painting so-called "portrait icons" which combined the realistic art of Western Europe with the traditions of Old-Russian painting. Quite a number of such portrait icons were created, representing prominent prelates of the church and royal personages. Well known, for example, is the portrait of *Tsar Feodor Ioanovich* and also the portrait of *Prince M. V. Skopin-Shuysky,* painted by a royal isographer in 1630 for the Prince's tomb in the Cathedral of the Archangel in the Moscow Kremlin. (Plates 102, 103)

In the second half of the seventeenth century, a period which gave birth to the art of modern times, two lines of development could be discerned in Old-Russian painting: one stemmed from the work of Simon Ushakov, the other, from the Stroganov school.

102
Tsar Feodor Ioanovich.
(Portrait icon)
17th century

103
Prince M.V. Skopin-Shuysky.
(Portrait icon)
17th century

104
The Cathedral of the Assumption in the Kremlin, Moscow.

Prevailing in the former was a striving for a realistic portrayal of life, with outwardly authentic presentation. In the latter, there is narrativeness and effusiveness; the icons encompass numerous episodes, details and figures, and display ornamental refinement.

In seventeenth century painting, the artistic image lost its former monumental, epic character. Icons became small in size, similar to an object that can be held in one's hand, examined on a church lectern or in small Old-Believers' oratories and prayer houses. Icon painters began to concentrate attention mainly on an icon's decoration.

At a time when icon painting in the capital was experiencing a decline, the Russian North, the Volga Region and the Rostov-Suzdal area produced icons which not only remained true to local traditions, but also to the traditions of Old-Russian painting.

*105
St. Nicholas the Miracle-Worker. Riza of gilt silver and enamel
18th century

Yaroslavl

Beginning from the mid-sixteenth century Yaroslavl, a vigorous trading town on the Volga river, turned into one of the country's leading cultural centers. In the second half of the seventeenth century there began the rapid construction of stone churches, as well as an accompanying expansion of the pictorial arts. Numerous quite unique cycles of church murals appeared and monumental iconostases were made by the best Yaroslavl and Kostroma masters. An icon-painting school of its own began evolving in Yaroslavl in the mid-sixteenth century. But it was under the strong influence of the Moscow Kremlin's Armory which effectively controlled the country's entire artistic life throughout the seventeenth century. Scores of Yaroslavl icon painters were summoned to the capital "on urgent state business."

The biographical icon was developed in Yaroslavl in a truly unique manner, with a stately-monumental treatment of the center-piece and a most detailed narrative in the marginal scenes. Some of the biographical icons had hundreds of such marginal scenes, crowded with thousands of miniature figures, and they were by no means inferior to the best icons of the Stroganov school.

Held in high esteem among Yaroslavl icon painters was Semyon Spiridonov of Kholmogory, an elegant and refined miniature painter, who excelled in painting with gold. Skillfully applied gold assist permeated the icon's entire painted area. The master gilded the crowns of the trees and intertwining branches, traced

106
The Venerated Paphnutius of Borovsk. Riza of silver, filigree, enamel
18th century

107

whimsical lines on the folds of garments and placed gold ornaments on architectural details.

Yaroslavl was responsible for some of the best pages in the history of seventeenth century Russian art—in architecture as well as mural and icon painting.

Icon Painting in the 18th and 19th Centuries

The development of the "grand style" of Old-Russian painting came to an end at the turn of the eighteenth century. As aptly noted by the art historian V. Bryusova: "By the seventeenth century, Russian art became an arena of struggle between two cultures with the Westernizing trend gaining the upper hand early in the eighteenth." It has been customary to maintain that beginning from this turning point, icon painting became a handicraft, yet Russian icon painting, in spite of the lowering of its artistic standards in general, in individual specimens and in certain stylistic trends, retained and developed the features of scholarly icon painting. The Westernizing influences of the eighteenth century were unable to uproot the national tradition, firmly entrenched

107
The Ship of Faith or the Church Persecuted.
17th-18th century

*108
St. Barbara, Martyr.
Second half of 18th century

109

The art of Palekh is characterized by fine miniature painting; it abounds in fairy-tale subjects, and features exotic plants and flowers. A finely woven herbaceous ornament usually covered all the garments of the saints, architectural details and margins of the icon.

in Russia, of a creative approach to the matter of icon painting as an exhalted art. The eminent Russian art historian V. Nikolsky wrote in this connection: "The icon has always resolutely preserved the unity of its inherent world and content, doing so with equal force and fury whether in the creations of first rate masters or in the works coming from less experienced hands, or even in second and third rate specimens."

In the eighteenth and nineteenth centuries Russian culture was divided. On one side was "metropolitan", academic art, and on the other, painting in the Russian provinces which carried on the basic icon-painting traditions.

Palekh, Mstera, Kholui, Shuya, Murom

The Beheading of St. John the Baptist.
Detail
Plate 113
Page 121

At the largest centers of handicraft icon production in Palekh, Mstera, Shuya, Kholui and Murom, and in the Russian North, icon painting retained its viability and went on developing in a creative manner throughout the entire eighteenth and early-nineteenth century.

In Mstera, Shuya and Kholui, situated close to navigable rivers and within easy reach of the frequently held fairs, icons were painted mainly for the market-place. They were relatively inexpensive and, with some exceptions, the standard was not high, for they were produced as fast as possible.

In Palekh, which was hard to reach because of bad roads and impenetrable forests, the old icon-painting traditions were retained. The Palekh artists, highly skilled masters, painted icons to order during spells of time free from field work, mainly in winter, just as peasants painted their distaffs and did their wood carving. Hence they regarded their work as applied art. They worked in their homes, unhurriedly, involving the entire family. The icons were good, solid and costly, catering mostly to Old Believers who collected specimens of Old-Russian painting. Together with ancient originals, the art of icon painting was handed down from father to son, from family to family, from generation to generation. The art of Palekh is characterized by fine miniature painting, and abounds in fairytale subjects and features exotic plants and flowers. A finely woven herbaceous ornament usually covered all the garments of the saints, architectural details and margins of the icon. In the eighteenth century Palekh evolved a peculiar icon-painting style, which combined a "Stroganov-type" with seventeenth century icon-painting techniques.

*109
The Presentation in the Temple.
Palekh
First half of 19th century

*110
Four-part icon: The Creation, The Only-Begotten Son of God, The Martyrs of Kizik. The Seven Sleepers of Ephesus. Palekh
19th century

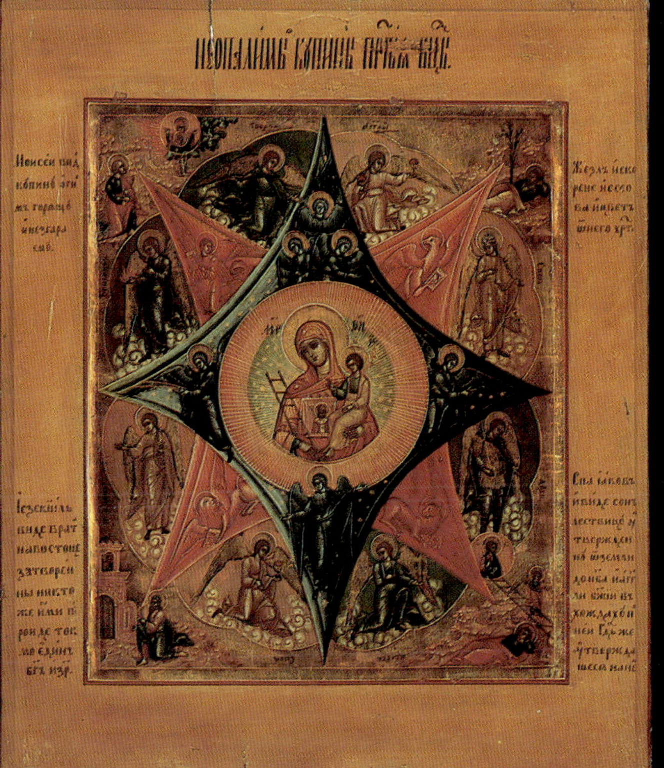

111

112

113

*111
Our Lady of the Burning Bush that Was Not Consumed.
Palekh
Mid-19th century

*112
Annunciation of the Conception of St. John the Baptist. Palekh
Late 19th-early 20th century

*113
The Beheading of St. John the Baptist. Palekh
19th century

Towards the middle of the nineteenth century, owing to the general decline in icon painting, the number of family-type icon-painting craftsmen steadily dwindled. Icon making fell into the hands of individual entrepreneurs who opened icon-painting workshops which employed virtually the entire population of the village. Because of low payment for icon-painting, the quality became worse and worse. The expression "We paint according to the price" became widespread.

After the revolution, the traditional icon-making craft of the Palekh craftsmen did not perish. The former icon-making workshops started a new kind of applied-art production–the painting of lacquer miniatures on papier-mâché, which has made Palekh famous not only throughout Russia, but far beyond its borders.

*114
St. Maxim the Greek.
Second half of 18th century

Icons of the North

Russia's North was a veritable preserve where this ancient culture and art was kept alive until the early twentieth century. Separated by dense forests and boundless expanses from major urban centers, it kept intact not only the poetic traditions of remote pagan beliefs and the heroic legends that came down from Kievan Russian times, but also the modest icons surviving in wooden churches and chapels, which are so touchingly naive and spontaneous. E. Smirnova, an expert on the art of the Russian North, writes: "The painting of the North is, in the last analysis, a peasant art, the art of 'peasant Russia'. It provides a glimpse into the art world of remote villages, and at works of art, other than icons, that hardly survive from pre-Peter the Great times. This 'wooden' art could hardly fail to leave its mark on the history of Russian culture, for it was an organic part of it–its most grassroots, folkloric layer."

An eighteenth century icon represents St. Maxim, the Greek, a philosopher and man of letters who lived in the sixteenth century. The laconic treatment and perfect composition are intended to convey the sequestered world of the Greek philosopher. Before the rise of Moscow, which systematically began to absorb independent principalities, the artistic life in Russia was scattered, with each town clinging to its own traditions and way of life. This is true of Vladimir, Rostov, Tver, Nizhni Novgorod, Yaroslavl. At different developmental stages they played either a greater or lesser role, but they could never rival Novgorod, Pskov and Moscow in the realm of culture.

The eighteenth century icons of *St. George and the Dragon* and *St. Maxim the Greek,* and the nineteenth century icon *Deposition in the Sepulcher* reflect the most characteristic features of Northern painting. The image of St. George remained the favorite hero in Russian icon painting until the twentieth century. In the sixteenth century a mounted St. George was the emblem of Grand-Ducal Moscow and later was included in the capital's coat-of-arms and that of the Russian empire.

*115
Deposition in the Sepulcher.
Early 19th century

*116
The Penitent Thief in Paradise.
18th century

*117
St. George and the Dragon.
18th century

15

116

117

118

No less interesting is the icon *Deposition in the Sepulcher*, where the huge figure of the Virgin, filling nearly all the icon's surface, seems to emphasize the immeasurable bereavement of the Mother of God as compared to that of the apostles surrounding Christ's dead body. (Plate 115)

Primitive icons made by village painters were widespread in the nineteenth century not in the Russian North alone, but also in other remote areas of "peasant Russia". Peasant religious art was closely interwoven with folkloric poetry, with an earthly and "pagan" presentation of heavenly subjects and a simplicity and spontaneity typical of folk art.

Along with the eighteenth and nineteenth century peasant icons, there were icons of the so-called "monastic brush". They were painted at a higher technical level, which depended both on the professional standards of the monastic workshops in general, as well as on the skills of its individual masters in particular.

Towards the end of the eighteenth century, when oil painting became fashionable, icon painters attempted to combine elements of traditional iconic techniques with the provincial portrait, so that at a certain level the line of demarcation between cultic and secular art became obliterated in both subject matter and style.

118
VASILI SURIKOV
Red Corner in a Peasant House.

Icon painting of the seventeenth and eighteenth centuries rounds out the centuries-long developmental period of Old-Russian painting, and emerges on the threshold of the realistic art of modern time.

Russian academic-pictorial art of the eighteenth and nineteenth centuries, though a far cry from icon-painting, had certain aesthetic factors in common. Many prominent academicians painted icons, frescoes and pictures on religious themes. The famous portrait painter D. Levitsky, together with A. Antropov, the chief painter of the Holy Synod, painted for the St. Andreas Cathedral in Kiev. V. Borovikovsky painted a great number of icons. An outstanding Russian painter, Alexander Ivanov, apart from the famous picture *Christ Appearing before the People,* did 247 water-colors and monochrome compositions on biblical themes. Taking part in painting for the St. Vladimir Cathedral built in Kiev were the artists V. Vasnetsov, M. Nesterov and M. Vrubel. I. Repin, N. Ghe, V. Polenov and many others painted religious subjects.

119
ILYA REPIN
A Religious Procession in the Province of Kursk.

Toward the turn of the twentieth century Old-Russian painting was downgraded to the level of a handicraft. "Icono-daubers", having changed over to oils, oblivious of the "original prototypes", took every license, guided mainly by their own fancy. Their cheap, coarse panels, intended for the populace, were sometimes called "pictorial " or "colored" or "red". In some towns "icon factories" were organized, i.e. simply large-scale workshops employing painter craftsmen and mass-producing cheap icons of low quality, where wood was replaced by cardboard, paper and tin, and the image was simply printed in a printing house.

So-called "sub-riza" icons appeared, where the painters rendered, in the academic manner, nothing but what remained uncovered by the riza. Jewelry began to displace painting. Inexpensive copper and silver-plated rizas with diverse plant ornamentation were stamped by machine. When specially commissioned, well-known jewelers' establishments in Moscow and St. Petersburg made silver and gold rizas with polychrome enameling, precious stones and pearls. Such rizas were sometimes magnificent objects of the jewelers' art in their own right.

120
A Religious Procession.
Detail
Plate 119
Page 125

*121
The Virgin of Tenderness.
Oklad–gilt silver, filigree,
enamel
19th century; Oklad–1908

*122
The Virgin of the Don. Riza–gilt silver, semiprecious stones

The Rediscovery of Old Russian Painting

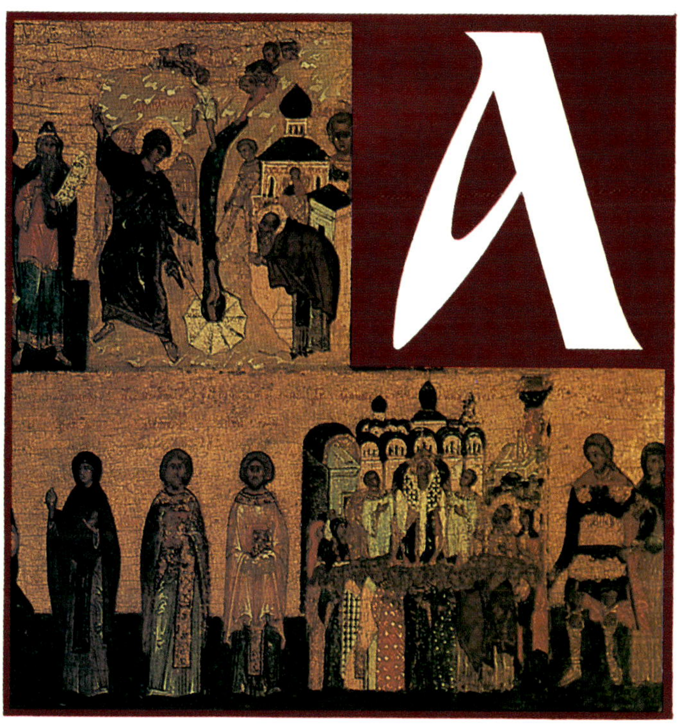

At the turn of the twentieth century the importance of icon painting in Russia was limited to its cultic function. Ancient icons, mainly of interest to Old-Believer collectors, became great rarities. According to M. Muratov, one of the first investigators of Old-Russian painting: "As early as the eighteenth century iconostases in the baroque and classicist styles replaced, wherever possible, the ancient ones of Novgorod and Muscovy. Old icons were relegated to church cellars or bell towers. Overpainted and distorted, they could be found only in foresaken remote towns...Old icons disappeared altogether from landlord estates...A sixteenth or even seventeenth century icon surviving within some noble family is a tremendous rarity."

The true face of an icon, its painting, the spiritual essence of this unique art, was concealed under layers of darkened varnish and later overpaintings. Russian icon painters who varnished their icons could hardly know that with time, under the effect of soot from candles and icon-lamps, they would darken so much as to virtually blacken out the original painting. So an icon had to be "freshened up". The new icon painter produced a new work, which expressed not only the aesthetic views of his time, but his personal tastes as well. At times the original image of ancient icons was discovered under five or six layers of subsequent overpaintings. It can be stated without exaggeration that not a single ancient icon has come down to us without at least partial restoration or complete overpaintings made in subsequent centuries. Moreover, most of the icons were covered by precious rizas and trimmings, and the dark faces of the saints gave precious little clue as to what the original painting was like under the *riza*.

Covered by heavy *rizas*, hidden under dense layers of varnish, the amazing creations of ancient Russian artists seemed doomed to oblivion forever. But early in the twentieth century a major event took place in the history of Russian art—the rediscovery of Old-Russian painting.

A magnificent five-tier Iconostasis is incorporated into this painting.

123
STEPAN SHUKHVOSTOV
Mass at the Annunciation Cathedral, Moscow.

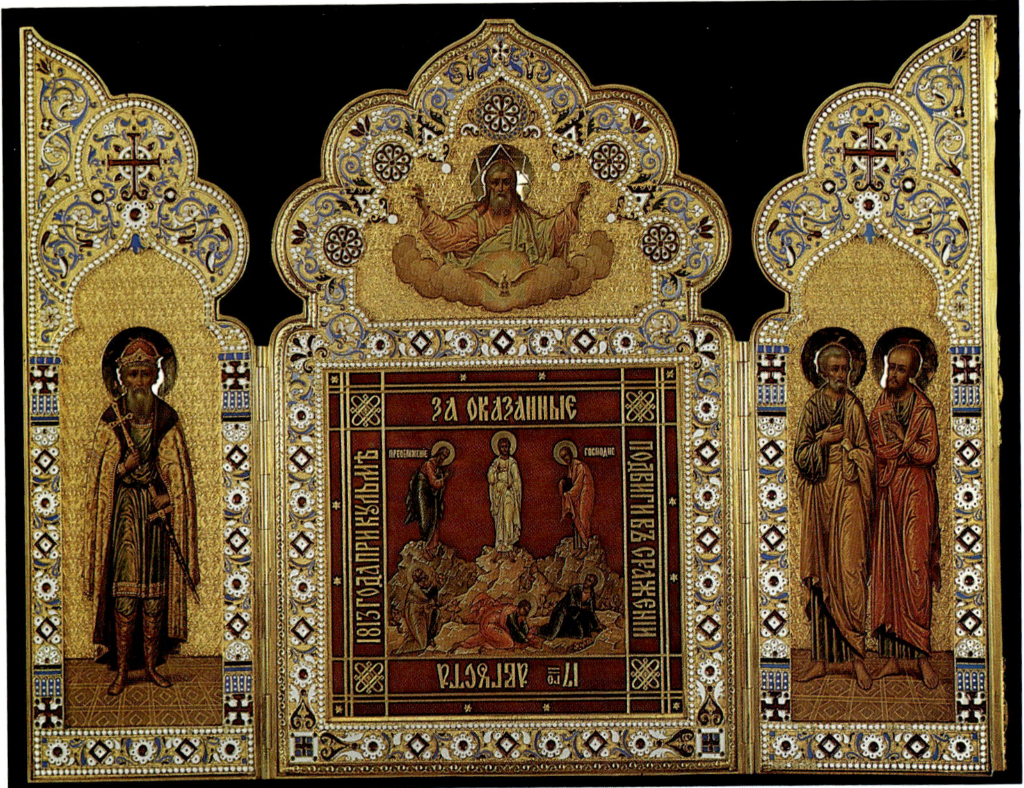

124

In 1904 the icon painter Guryanov was commissioned by the monks of the St. Sergius Monastery of the Trinity, to clean Rublev's icon of the Trinity from age-long soot and dirt. The cleaning process was like a miracle. The black film of varnish disappeared, revealing the well preserved paints—fresh, bright and vibrant. It was as though time imparted some special strength to them. From this point on vigorous collecting and restoration of Russian icons began. The collections of N.P. Likhachev and I.S. Ostroukhov laid the foundations of the present collections of Old-Russian art at the Tretyakov Gallery and the Russian Museum.

The first exhibition of icons from private collections was opened in Petrograd in 1911 during an artists' congress, and another was held in Moscow in 1913. These exhibitions were very important for the realization of the aesthetic merits of the Russian icon. According to V. Lazarev: "The spectators seemed suddenly freed from a screen which had obscured the true face of Russian painting. Instead of dark, gloomy icons covered by a thick layer of varnish, they saw beautiful works of art that could have honored any nation...It became at once clear that this was an art that was neither ascetic, austere, nor fanatical, that it vividly reflected a living popular art, that by its lucidity and the special clarity of its structural forms it reflected back to the painting of antiquity; to be regarded as one of the most perfect manifestations of Russian genius."

124
Three-Leaf Folding Icon.
Silver, filigree, enamel
Ovchinnikov

The aesthetic merits of Old-Russian painting, developed over many centuries, manifested themselves not only in the best religious panel painting of the past, but also in the work of twentieth-century artists.

After the 1913 exhibition in Moscow many painters of the Russian avant-garde fell under the spell of the Russian icon—Natalia Goncharova, Vladimir Tatlin and Marc Chagal among them. A major icon collector in our time, the painter Pavel Korin, himself descended from a family of icon-painting peasants of the Palekh village, believed that "without traditions and continuity there can be no art, no innovation." He used many icon-painting techniques in his own pictures, mosaics and stained-glass compositions.

In the nineteenth century so-called "sub-riza" icons appeared. In these the painters rendered nothing but what remained uncovered by the *riza.* When specially commissioned, well-known jewelers' establishments in Moscow and St. Petersburg made silver and gold *rizas*, with polychrome enameling, precious stones and pearls. Such *rizas* often proved first-class objects of the jewelers' art in their own right.

125

*125
The Virgin of Kazan.
Riza-silver, engraving, filigree, enamel, pearls
1899

*126
The Virgin of Kazan.
Riza–silver, filigree, enamel
19th century

*127
The Virgin of Vladimir.
Riza-gilt, enamel
19th century

128

*128
Our Lady of the Burning Bush that Was Not Consumed, and All Other Images of the Virgin with Festivals.
19th century

129

130

After seeing the Novgorodian icons in I.S. Ostroukhov's collection, the French painter Henri Matisse said: "This is truly national art, the prime source of artistic exploration... everywhere the same vividness and manifestation of great emotional strength..."

In the past half century, much has been done in the Soviet Union towards the discovery, restoration and protection of these monuments of culture. In 1944 a major art restoration center was opened in Moscow and in recent decades hundreds of first-rate Russian icons from the twelfth to the eighteenth century have been found and restored, so that the collections in the Russian Museum in Leningrad and the Tretyakov Gallery in Moscow have been expanded considerably. The third exhibition (after those of 1911 and 1913) of Old-Russian painting of the thirteenth to eighteenth centuries from private collections in Moscow, Leningrad and Tallin was held in 1974 in the halls of the Andrei Rublev Museum of Old Russian Art, newly opened in Moscow in 1960.

Old-Russian painting is a natural link between modern man and the countless riches of the spiritual culture of the past. Today many Russian icons have won their well-deserved place among the world's greatest masterpieces.

*129
Christ in Majesty.
Riza–silver, enamel
19th century

*130
St. Nicholas the Miracle-Worker. Riza–silver, enamel
19th century

List of Plates

All sizes are in centimeters

Plate numbers shown with an asterisk (*) are published here for the first time.

1
Winter Landscape with Church in thc Town of Suzdal.

2
The Virgin of Vladimir.
First half of 12th century
Tretyakov Gallery, Moscow
113.5 x 68

3
The Apostles Peter and Paul.
Mid-11th century
Museum of History and Architecture, Novgorod
236 x 147

4
St. Nicholas the Miracle-Worker.
Early 13th century
Tretyakov Gallery, Moscow
145 x 94

5
St. George.
Early 12th century
Tretyakov Gallery, Moscow
230 x 142

6
The Ustyug Annunciation.
Second half of 12th century
Tretyakov Gallery, Moscow
229 x 144

7
The Virgin Orans.
Circa 1224
Tretyakov Gallery, Moscow
194 x 120

8
The Virgin Orans.
Detail

9
The Prophet Elijah.
First half of 15th century
Tretyakov Gallery, Moscow
75 x 57

10
Descent of the Holy Ghost.
15th century
Museum of History and Architecture, Novgorod
75 x 55

11
The Virgin of the Sign with Selected Saints (Barlaam of Khutyn, John the Almsgiver, Paraskeva Pyatnitsa and Anastasia).
Early 15th century
Russian Museum, Leningrad
66 x 50

12
The Virgin of the Sign with Selected Saints (the Prophet Elijah, Paraskeva Pyatnitsa, Nicholas the Miracle-Worker, Blaise, Florus and Laurus).
Second quarter of 15th century
Tretyakov Gallery, Moscow
69 x 57

13
SS. Florus and Laurus.
Late 15th century
Tretyakov Gallery, Moscow
47 x 37

*14
The Assembly of the Twelve Apostles.
First half of 15th century
Museum of History and Architecture, Novgorod
133 x 95.5

15
St. George and the Dragon.
Late 14th-early 15th century
Russian Museum, Leningrad
58 x 41.5

*16
The Virgin of Mercy.
First half of 16th century
Private collection, Moscow
45 x 38

17
SS. Blaise and Spyridon.
Circa 1407
Historical Museum, Moscow
117.5 x 85.5

18
St. George with Scenes from His Life.
Early 14th century
Russian Museum, Leningrad
89 x 63

19
Battle between the Novgorodians and the Suzdalians.
Circa 1460
Museum of History and Architecture, Novgorod
165 x 120

20
The Virgin of the Don.
Circa 1390
Tretyakov Gallery, Moscow
86 x 68

21
The Dormition (on the reverse of the Virgin of the Don).
Circa 1390
Tretyakov Gallery, Moscow
86 x 68

22
The Last Judgement.
Third quarter of 15th century
Tretyakov Gallery, Moscow
162 x 115

23
The Descent from the Cross.
Late 15th century
Tretyakov Gallery, Moscow
91 x 62

24
The Entombment.
Late 15th century
Tretyakov Gallery, Moscow
90 x 63

25
The Nativity of Christ with Selected Saints (Eudocia, John Climacus and Juliana).
First half of 15th century
Tretyakov Gallery, Moscow
57 x 42

26
St. Theodore Stratilates with Scenes from His Life.
Late 15th century
Museum of History and Architecture, Novgorod
136.5 x 109

*27
St. Nicetas Giving the Devil a Hiding, with Deesis and Selected Saints.
15th century
Private collection, Moscow
82 x 58

*28
The Nativity of the Virgin with Scenes from Her Life.
Late 15th century
Art Restoration Workshops, Novgorod
168 x 115

29
The Prophets Daniel, David and Solomon.
Circa 1497
Tretyakov Gallery, Moscow
67 x 179

*30
St. Nicholas the Miracle-Worker.
Late 15th century
Art Museum of the Karelian Autonomous Soviet Socialist Republic, Petrozavodsk
109 x 88

*31
Deesis Tier, Seven Full-Length Figures.
First half of 14th century
Art Museum of the KarASSR, Petrozavodsk
62 x 86

*32
The Prophet Elijah in the Desert.
Late 15th-early 16th century
Art Museum of the KarASSR, Petrozavodsk
57 x 42

*33
Patria.
Late 15th-early 16th century
Art Museum of the KarASSR, Petrozavodsk
135 x 96

34
The Prophets Daniel, David and Solomon.
Detail.

35
The Archangel Gabriel.
First half of 15th century
Russian Museum, Leningrad
104 x 63

*36
St. Nicholas the Miracle-Worker with Scenes from His Life.
Second half of 16th century
Art Museum, Pskov
99 x 77

37
The Nativity of Christ with Selected Saints.
Late 15th century
Russian Museum, Leningrad
81 x 71

38
Deesis.
13th century
Russian Museum, Leningrad
140 x 110

39
SS. Paraskeva Pyatnitsa, Gregory the Theologian, John Chrysostom and Basil the Great.
Early 15th century
Tretyakov Gallery, Moscow
147 x 134

40
SS. Paraskeva Pyatnitsa, Gregory the Theologian, John Chrysostom and Basil the Great. Detail

*41
Four-Part Icon: The Descent into Limbo, The Trinity, Three Selected Saints, and The Nativity of Christ.
Second half of 15th century
Private collection, Moscow
81 x 65

42
SS. Boris and Gleb.
Mid-14th century
Tretyakov Gallery, Moscow
128 x 75

43
DIONYSIUS
The Virgin Hodegetria.
1502
Russian Museum, Leningrad
141 x 106

44
Christ in Majesty.
Second half of 15th century
Tretyakov Gallery, Moscow
30 x 25

45
SS. Boris and Gleb with Scenes from Their Lives.
Second half of 15th century
Tretyakov Gallery, Moscow
134 x 89

46, 47, 48
Marginal Scenes of the Icon of SS. Boris and Gleb.

*49
The Virgin of Yaroslavl.
Second half of 15th century
Private collection, Moscow
63 x 51

*50
Paraskeva Pyatnitsa with Scenes from Her Life.
16th century
Private collection, Moscow
54 x 46

51
DIONYSIUS AND DISCIPLES
The Descent into Limbo.
1502
Russian Museum, Leningrad
137 x 99.5

52
School of **THEOPHANES THE GREEK**
The Transfiguration.
Circa 1403
Tretyakov Gallery, Moscow
184 x 134

53
ANDREI RUBLEV
The Saviour.
Circa 1410
Tretyakov Gallery, Moscow
158 x 108

54
ANDREI RUBLEV
The Apostle Paul.
Circa 1410
Tretyakov Gallery, Moscow
160 x 110

55
ANDREI RUBLEV
The Trinity.
Circa 1411
Tretyakov Gallery, Moscow
142 x 114

56, 57
ANDREI RUBLEV
The Trinity. Detail

58
DIONYSIUS
The Virgin Hodegetria.
1482
Tretyakov Gallery, Moscow
135 x 111

59
PROCHORUS OF GORODETS
The Last Supper.
1405
Cathedral of the Annunciation. The Kremlin, Moscow
80 x 61

60
DIONYSIUS' Workshop.
St. Cyril of Byelozersk with Scenes from His Life.
Late 15th century
Russian Museum, Leningrad
152 x 117

61
DIONYSIUS
The Crucifixion.
1500
Tretyakov Gallery, Moscow
85 x 52

62
The Dormition.
Circa 1497
Tretyakov Gallery, Moscow
145 x 115

63
DIONYSIUS' Workshop
In Thee Rejoiceth.
Early 16th century
Tretyakov Gallery, Moscow
146 x 110

64
The Dormition. Detail

65
In Thee Rejoiceth. Detail

66
The Monastery of the Intercession at Suzdal.

*67
17th-Century iconostasis.
Ecclesiastical Academy, St. Sergius Monastery of The Trinity, Zagorsk

*68-78
Festive Tier from the Iconostasis of the Cathedral of the Assumption at Sviyazhsk. Mid-16th century

68 **The Annunciation.**
65 x 54
69 **The Nativity of Christ.**
65 x 54
70 **Presentation of Christ in the Temple.**
65 x 54
71 **The Baptism of Christ.**
65 x 54
72 **The Raising of Lazarus.**
65 x 54
73 **Entry into Jerusalem.**
65 x 54
74 **The Transfiguration.**
65 x 54
75 **The Trinity.**
65 x 54
76 **The Incredulity of Thomas.**
65 x 54
77 **The Descent of the Holy Ghost.**
65 x 54
78 **The Raising of the Cross.**
65 x 54

*79-88
Deesis Tier from the Iconostasis of the Cathedral of the Assumption at Sviyazhsk. Mid-16th century

79 **St. John Chrysostom.**
149 x 53
80 **St. Basil the Great.**
149 x 53
81 **The Apostle Peter.**
149 x 53
82 **The Archangel Michael.**
149 x 53
83 **The Virgin.**
149 x 53
84 **Christ in Majesty.**
149 x 107
85 **St. John the Baptist.**
149 x 53
86 **The Archangel Gabriel.**
149 x 53
87 **The Apostle Paul.**
149 x 53
88 **St. Nicholas the Miracle-Worker.**
149 x 53

89
St. Hypatius of Gangra with Scenes from His Life.
First half of 15th century
Tretyakov Gallery, Moscow
112 x 81

*90
Apostle Paul from a Deesis Tier.
Second half of 15th century
Private collection, Moscow
80 x 32

*91
The Nativity of the Virgin.
16th century
Private collection, Moscow
80 x 54

*92
Lives of the Saints for November.
16th century
Tretyakov Gallery, Moscow
56 x 45

93
Lives of the Saints. Detail

94
Cathedral of the Intercession–Church of St. Basil the Blessed.
16th century
Red Square, Moscow

*95
SS. Procopius and John of Ustyug. Silver Oklad
17th century
Historical Museum, Moscow
35 x 30.5

96
Three-Leaf Folding Icon (without central portion).
17th century
Historical Museum, Moscow
13.5 x 33.5 (each leaf)

97
PROCOPIUS CHIRIN
St. John the Baptist–Angel of the Desert.
17th century
Tretyakov Gallery, Moscow
37 x 31

*98
The Virgin of the Sign with Scenes from Her Life.
Second half of 17th century
Historical Museum, Moscow
156 x 141

99
SIMON USHAKOV
The Vernicle (The Saviour Not Painted by Hand).
17th century
Historical Museum, Moscow
54 x 43.5

100
The Last Judgement.
17th century
Museum of Old Russian Painting, Yaroslavl
97 x 72

101
The Vision of Sexton Tarasius.
Late 17th-early 18th century
Tretyakov Gallery, Moscow
90 x 70

102
Tsar Feodor Ioanovich. (Portrait icon)
17th century
Historical Museum, Moscow
42 x 32

103
Prince M.V. Skopin-Shuysky. (Portrait icon)
17th century
Historical Museum, Moscow
40 x 34

104
The Cathedral of the Assumption in the Kremlin, Moscow.

*105
St. Nicholas the Miracle-Worker. Riza of gilt silver and enamel
18th century
Historical Museum, Moscow
33 x 26.5

106
The Venerated Paphnutius of Borovsk. Riza of silver, filigree, enamel.
18th century
Historical Museum, Moscow
33 x 27.5

107
The Ship of Faith or the Church Persecuted.
17th-18th century
Tretyakov Gallery, Moscow
64 x 92

*108
St. Barbara, Martyr.
Second half of 18th century
Historical Museum, Moscow
107 x 64

*109
The Presentation in the Temple.
First half of 19th century
Palekh
Church Archeology Exhibition Room, (CAER), Moscow Ecclesiastical Academy, Zagorsk
35 x 29

*110
Four-part icon: The Creation, The Only-Begotten Son of God, The Martyrs of Kizik. The Seven Sleepers of Ephesus. Palekh
19th century
CAER, Moscow Ecclesiastical Academy, Zagorsk
35 x 29

*111
Our Lady of the Burning Bush that Was Not Consumed.
Palekh
Mid-19th century
Historical Museum, Moscow
31.5 x 26.5

*112
Annunciation of the Conception of St. John the Baptist. Palekh
Late 19th-early 20th century
Historical Museum, Moscow
32 x 27

*113
The Beheading of St. John the Baptist. Palekh
19th century
Historical Museum, Moscow
33 x 28

*114
St. Maxim the Greek.
Second half of 18th century
Private collection, Moscow
24 x 30

*115
Deposition in the Sepulcher.
Early 19th century
Private collection, Moscow
65 x 51

*116
The Penitent Thief in Paradise.
18th century
Private collection, Moscow
50 x 150

*117
St. George and the Dragon.
18th century
Private collection, Moscow
108 x 130

118
VASILI SURIKOV
Red Corner in a Peasant House.
1880
23 x 34

119
ILYA REPIN
A Religious Procession in the Province of Kursk.
1880-1883
175 x 280

120
A Religious Procession.
Detail

*121
The Virgin of Tenderness.
Oklad–gilt silver, filigree, enamel
19th century; Oklad–1908
Historical Museum, Moscow
27 x 31

*122
The Virgin of the Don. Riza–gilt silver, semiprecious stones
19th century
CAER, Moscow Ecclesiastical Academy, Zagorsk
32.5 x 27

123
STEPAN SHUKHVOSTOV
Mass at the Annunciation Cathedral, Moscow.
187 x 144

124
Three-Leaf Folding Icon.
Silver, filigree, enamel by Ovchinnikov
Historical Museum, Moscow
39.6 x 44.8

*125
The Virgin of Kazan.
Riza–silver, engraving, filigree, enamel, pearls
1899
Historical Museum, Moscow
27 x 34

*126
The Virgin of Kazan.
Riza–silver, filigree, enamel
19th century
Historical Museum, Moscow
27.5 x 29

*127
The Virgin of Vladimir.
Riza-gilt, enamel
19th century
Private collection, New York
126 x 95.5

*128
Our Lady of the Burning Bush that Was Not Consumed, and All Other Images of the Virgin with Festivals.
19th century
CAER, Moscow Ecclesiastical Academy, Zagorsk
109 x 96

*129
Christ in Majesty.
Riza–silver, enamel
19th century
Private collection, New York
27 x 31

*130
St. Nicholas the Miracle-Worker. Riza—silver, enamel
19th century
Private collection, New York
27 x 31

Printed by Frank C. Toole & Sons, Inc., Farmingdale, New York